More Tales For The Masses

Stories Connecting Scripture
And Everyday Life

Timothy E. Healy

CSS Publishing Company, Inc.
Lima, Ohio

MORE TALES FOR THE MASSES

FIRST EDITION
Copyright © 2023
by CSS Publishing Co., Inc.

Published by CSS Publishing Company, Inc., Lima, Ohio 45807. All rights reserved. No part of this publication may be reproduced in any manner whatsoever without the prior permission of the publisher, except in the case of brief quotations embodied in critical articles and reviews. Inquiries should be addressed to: CSS Publishing Company, Inc., Permissions Department, 5450 N. Dixie Highway, Lima, Ohio 45807.

Scripture texts in this work are taken from the *New American Bible* with Revised New Testament and Revised Psalms © 1991, 1986, 1970 Confraternity of Christian Doctrine, Washington, D.C. and are used by permission of the copyright owner. All Rights Reserved. No part of the *New American Bible* may be reproduced in any form without permission in writing from the copyright owner.

Library of Congress Cataloging-in-Publication Data

Names: Healy, Timothy E., author.
Title: More tales for the masses : stories connecting scripture and everyday life / Timothy E. Healy.
Description: First edition. | Lima, Ohio : CSS Publishing Company, Inc., [2022] | Includes index.
Identifiers: LCCN 2022027252 (print) | LCCN 2022027253 (ebook) | ISBN 9780788030727 | ISBN 9780788030734 (adobe pdf)
Subjects: LCSH: Homiletical illustrations. | Storytelling--Religious aspects--Christianity.
Classification: LCC BV4225.3 .H428 2022 (print) | LCC BV4225.3 (ebook) | DDC 251/.08--dc23/eng/20220815
LC record available at https://lccn.loc.gov/2022027252
LC ebook record available at https://lccn.loc.gov/2022027253

For more information about CSS Publishing Company resources, visit our website at www.csspub.com, email us at csr@csspub.com, or call (800) 241-4056.

e-book:
ISBN-13: 978-0-7880-3073-4
ISBN-10: 0-7880-3073-6

ISBN-13: 978-0-7880-3072-7
ISBN-10: 0-7880-3072-8   PRINTED IN USA

Contents

Introduction	7
Stories	9
Hospice Visit	11
Snakes	14
Messages And Messengers	17
Forgiving Enemies	20
Abuse	23
Joy And Happiness	27
Servant Leadership	30
Wisdom	33
The Good Shepherd	36
Exorcism	40
Where Was God?	43
It's Not Fair!	46
Transfiguration	49
You Look Just Like Jesus	53
Blindness	56
Blessing	59
Miracle	61
Aneurysm	63
Chosen	65
Satisfaction Of The Deepest Longing	68
Taz	72
Palm Sunday	76
Making A Name For Yourself	80
Cannibals, Magic, and Real Presence	84
Digital Possession	88
Pinocchio	92
Your Worst Nightmare	96
Repentance	99
Trinity	103

Hide And Seek	106
Unclean	109
Ray	113
How To Listen To A Bad Homily	117
The First Eucharist Quiz	125
Poems	129
Weeding	131
Pain	133
Midnight In My Daughter's qOld Room	134
Landing Soon	136
Waterfall	138
I Met My Neighbor At His Place	139
Infant Baptism	140
Learning To Center	142
Visiting Your Grave	144
The Pantheon	145
Psalm 139 From Another Point Of View	147
Secrets	149
The Anchor	150
On The Trail	152
The Smartest Guy In The Room	154
Parables	157
The Parable Of The Bowl	159
The Parable Of The Puzzle	161
Blurbularia	165
Euphonium	167
Calling Jesus	169
How Does Your Garden Grow?	170
Let Go	171
Father Damien	173
Peek-a-boo	175
The Wish	177
Denial	179
Fathers' Day — Happy Birthday!	181

Gardening	183
Mint	185
Gravitationally Challenged	187
Being A Deacon	189
Grandparents	191
Christmas Gifts	193
Compassion	195
Mistaken Identities	197
Silence	199
Recognizing Yourself	201
Confirmation Interviews	203
Situational Awareness	205
Excess	207
Amnesia	209
Fear	211
Teaching	213
A Very Special Gift	215
New Year's Resolutions	217
Acceptance	219
Harmony	221
Something Big	223
Familiarity	225
The Forgotten Icon	227
Music	231
Index	233

Introduction

The purpose of this book is to help you to love and to be loved. That is, after all, the first and greatest commandment, wouldn't you agree?

More Tales for the Masses continues where *Tales for the Masses* left off, with some additional material in different genres. In this book you'll find some poetry, challenging reflection questions and more. The bulk of the book consists of stories that connect scripture with everyday life, largely taken from homilies I've given over the years.

As always, the stories are true tales that may or may not actually have happened quite that way. None is about any particular person, but many are about lots of people in general. The book is designed to be useful for people who enjoy *lectio divina*, small Christian communities and similar devotional groups. The previous volume found a home in groups of other religious traditions, and hopefully this one will as well.

Thanks belong to the usual suspects — my wife and family, friends, co-religionists, everyone at the hospitals and other venues at which I've worked or volunteered, and the parishes to which I've been assigned. Special thanks to Deacon Bob Blair, who inspired me to become a deacon in the first place, and his lovely wife, Elaine, who taught my own wonderful wife, Chris, how to keep me in line. Special thanks to the Treacy family for permitting me to tell you the story of Taz, the resurrection cat.

Thanks, of an entirely different sort are due to Mark Pickett, who took the amazing photograph that accompanies *Transfiguration*. What you see there is the picture he took on his iPhone; it has not been altered in any way from the moment he took it. Special thanks to Gary Balich and his lovely wife, Judy, along with Mark Hamel, who kindly read the book in its earliest forms, and John Gueil, whose wisdom and suffering saturate these pages. They caught several errors and helped make the book so much better for you in so many ways!

Reflection questions for the original *Tales for the Masses* can be found at http://www.talesforthemasses.com. Permission is granted to download them freely for personal, noncommercial use.

Stories

With few exceptions, all of the stories in this section came from homilies delivered over the last few years. In some cases, I've included the entire homily, since the story by itself would lack sufficient context. I hope that you enjoy reading the stories, the background scripture (see the appendix for a cross-reference) and, if you happen to be a homilist too, that you can adapt one or more of these for your own use.

Hospice Visit

A few years ago, I was asked to spend some time with a man in the hospice unit within the hospital. Off I went, as always having no idea of what might happen next. God seems to like it that way.

I found a very thin man with skin yellowed by cancer, but alert and friendly. I introduced myself and invited him into conversation. He told me knew he was dying and was in fact going to leave the hospital later that day to go home for the last week or two of his life. No one was going to be there for him. Over the years he had alienated all his friends and just about all his family.

He told me he believed in God, but didn't belong to any church. He did want to pray though, so we said Psalm 23 together — the one that begins "The Lord is my shepherd…."

Then he began to tell me about his life; how he had suffered and caused plenty of suffering for others himself. At one point he turned towards me and asked me, with one of the saddest expressions I'd ever seen on another human being's face, if I thought God would send him to hell, almost as if he was expecting me to say, "Why of course, you miserable bum, why would you think otherwise?"

That's not what I told him though, and I believe most of you wouldn't have said so either. Instead, I told him that God knows what God has made, loves us and is compassionate with all of us in our suffering — both that suffering which afflicts us and also that which we cause. I'm not good at memorizing, but there are a couple of psalms I do remember, and they came in handy just then.

"The Lord is kind and full of compassion, it says in Psalm 145," I told him. "Slow to anger and abounding in love. How good is the Lord to all. Compassionate to all his creatures."

He liked that and asked for more, so I read him the part of Psalm 103 that folks in situations like his are eager to hear. St. Hilary had written that "fear" of the Lord is properly understood as "love" of the Lord. When I recite it to people, I always make that substitution. It then reads like this:

"Bless the LORD, my soul; all my being, bless his holy name! Bless the LORD, my soul; who pardons all your sins and heals all your ills, who redeems your life from the pit, and crowns you with mercy and compassion...."

"Merciful and gracious is the LORD, slow to anger, abounding in mercy. He will not always accuse and nurses no lasting anger; He has not dealt with us as our sins merit, nor requited us as our wrongs deserve."

"For as the heavens tower over the earth, so his mercy towers over those who [love] him. As far as the east is from the west, so far has he removed our sins from us. As a father has compassion on his children, so the LORD has compassion on those who [love] him."

"For he knows how we are formed, remembers that we are dust. As for man, his days are like the grass; he blossoms like a flower in the field. A wind sweeps over it and it is gone; its place knows it no more. But the LORD's mercy is from age to age, toward those who [love] him...."[1]

I told him that was how Jesus treated people by and large during his ministry on Earth, setting an example for the rest of us to follow.

Would God send him to hell? I told him I didn't run the universe but wouldn't bet any money on that. Peter Kreeft, the theologian at Boston College, who wrote *Everything You Ever Wanted to Know about Heaven — But Never Dreamed of Asking*, had opined that there was only such a thing as heaven, I told him, and hell was that part of heaven occupied by people who really, really didn't want to be there. The fires of hell are the pains of shame, hatred and unforgiveness that we simply won't ever bring to God for healing.

He pondered all that, touched my hand, gave me a little smile and said "Thanks, you've given me hope."

I felt for all the world like one of those four guys who dropped their paralyzed friend in on Jesus and watched him be healed in body and spirit. My hospice friend had been paralyzed by fear and anxiety but ended up that day in a different spot.

---

1   Tim's rendition of Psalm 103, following St. Hilary's opinion that 'fear of God' means 'love of God'

It is an awesome thing to ride the wave of the compassion of God together with a person who is suffering. I left that room feeling like a minnow in a tidal wave. In that moment I felt a sense of the vastness of God's love flow from God, through me, over into this man who was soon to go home and die. In my heart I knew that although no one might be with him when he breathed his last, he wouldn't be alone. Jesus, he who relieves human suffering, the compassionate healer of hearts, would be right there with him.

Questions For Discussion

1. Read Psalms 23, 103, and 139. How do they make you feel? If you were ministering to another person, in what situations do you think these psalms might best apply?

2. In my chaplain work, everyone, and I mean *everyone* I have ever met who is dying, is of the opinion that they didn't do a very good job here and could have/should have and definitely would do much better if they had it all to do over again. How would you respond to a dying person's statement like that? What does your response tell you about your own situation?

Snakes

One of my friends did his graduate thesis in psychology on ophidiophobia. For those of you who have no idea what that is, ophidiophobia is the fear of snakes.

Charlie told me that the only way you could get folks to overcome their fear of snakes was to have them sit in a room with a snake or two and work their way up to getting them to touch and finally handle the snakes. When I asked him what the hardest part of the procedure was, he replied "Getting people into the room with the snakes to begin with."

It's like that with our most fundamental fears, too. Fear of death, fear of loss, fear of isolation and so on. I doubt that many of us want to skip cheerfully into the room with our snakes. But the only way around any fear is directly through it. Denial and avoidance are perfectly okay in the short term and might buy you some time to calm down, but in the end there's nothing for it except to take the plunge and confront those demons.

John's gospel contains a passage that compares Jesus on the cross to Moses raising the snake on a rod in front of the Israelites. The simple message is that to be healed, we must look at the very thing that is afflicting us. It's a hard thing to do, but sometimes the way we handle our fears and brokenness makes things harder than they need to be. Let me tell you a story and you can see if you agree.

Three young ladies were chatting in their dorm room in a college near here one evening not too long ago and the subject came up of the most trouble they'd gotten into as little kids.

"I was playing house with my friends one day and I took my father's wallet and keys down to the basement," said Annie. "We got busy with other things, and I forgot to put them back. Then I went over to one of my friends' houses to play. In the meantime, my father had a big meeting he was supposed to run down at the fire house, and he couldn't find his wallet or keys."

"He's got a short fuse even when he's happy, and he was yelling at my brothers and mom. He figured they had to have moved them, and of course they had no idea, and it couldn't have been me because I was playing over at Rachel's house. He ended up calling a friend and got to the meeting late. It didn't go well because he was mad and his friend wouldn't drive him home because he'd been insulted. My dad had to walk home, and when he got home it was even uglier than before. I was terrified to tell him I'd taken his keys and wallet."

"I waited until he stopped yelling and went upstairs and then snuck the wallet and keys back where they belonged. I hoped I could get away without being discovered, but my brother Timmy saw me and snitched, and boy did I get it! To this day we still talk about it, and part of me wonders whether my dad ever really forgave me. I wonder whether I've ever really forgiven myself or my miserable brother, either. I still feel awful about it."

"That's terrible, Annie," Joan said. "I left the bathtub running once, when I was ten, and then went to do something else and forgot the water was on. When I heard my mom and dad screaming from the kitchen downstairs, I wished I could become invisible. It was awful. My dad spent two weeks fixing everything up again. They still point out the part of the ceiling that doesn't look like the rest of it. I wish it had never happened — I can't seem to get past it. How about you Lisa?"

"Well, my brother and I were throwing rocks at each other one day and I tossed one and it hit the car and put a big dent in it. My brother gloated and told me I was dead, then ran in to tell my dad."

"My dad came out, looked at the car, looked at me, came over, took me by the hand and led me over to the car. Something about the way he took my hand told me he wasn't going to hurt me, so I didn't cry. He asked me to feel the dent and then asked me what it would be like if the dent was in my brother's head rather than in the car. His face and his tone of voice told me that he loved my brother and me, and that what we had both been doing was bad, because we could've hurt each other and if we did *that*, we'd be hurting him, too."

"Then he called my brother over and asked him the same question and we both realized in that moment that we had done what was wrong. Then he asked us what we thought should happen next. I told my brother I was sorry, and he said the same to me. Then my dad hugged us both, told us to go to our rooms for a half-hour and then we could come out."

"I asked about the dent. Dad looked at me, and then my brother and said 'You are more important to me than a dent in a fender, Lisa. The fender's just a thing. You're my son and daughter. I might like my fender and prefer it not to have a dent, but I love you and I'd rather have you understand right from wrong, know you're loved, and grow up without dents to your spirit, and without any desire to dent anyone else's, either. That's when I cried."

Annie and Joan looked at Lisa with long, sad glances and things got quiet for a moment. Finally, Joan said "I wish my dad was like your dad, Lisa," as Annie nodded silently. Lisa slowly smiled at her two friends and said "Oh, but he is!" and the two women grinned warmly at Lisa as it dawned on them what she'd really meant.

Questions For Discussion

1. Mercy is sometimes defined as overwhelming, undeserved kindness, freely given and way beyond anything we might ever have expected. Have you experienced or dispensed mercy like this in your life? What was it like for you? What response did you receive?

2. If God loves us unconditionally (and we have it on God's own word that God actually does), what impedes us from believing that we are loved and will be shown mercy?

Messages And Messengers

Many years ago, when the internet was still new and smartphones hadn't been invented, I attended a technology conference titled Advertising and the Internet. We were told that the average person received roughly 5,000 messages a day. The presenter said that included billboards, TV, radio, magazines and even comments from family and friends. The goal by 2015 was to raise that number to 15,000 messages a day. How well do you think they're doing?

Those numbers might not reflect everyone's experience accurately, but I think we can agree that we're all subjected to an enormous number of competing messages. How do we decide which are worthy of our attention and which are not?

In the early church, conflicting messages were circulating about who Jesus was and about the significance of his life and death. How could anyone back then have decided which were worthy of attention and which were not? Curiously, scripture seems to tell us that the flock back then just knew and suggests to us that such is true today as well. There's something that allows us to discern reliably what makes a message worthy of our attention. Let's take a look and see what it might be.

We'll start by considering the message itself. The complete Christian message is described in more detail than anyone would probably ever want to know in the Catechism of the Catholic Church. Happily, we don't have to read the whole thing to find out what it is about the message that makes it possible for us to discern that what we're heeding is indeed the voice of the Good Shepherd. Paragraph 25 of the Catechism says, "The whole concern of doctrine and its teaching must be directed to the love that never ends …so that anyone can see that all the works of perfect Christian virtue spring from love and have no other objective than to arrive at love."[2] Clearly, if the messages we hear are about love, then it's the Good Shepherd's voice we're hearing.

---

[2] *Catechism of the Catholic Church*: Second Edition (Washington, D.C.: United States Catholic Conference, 1997), 12.

That's surely a good start, but as the famous Canadian Catholic academic Marshall McLuhan pointed out years ago, "the medium is the message,"[3] and that's as true of the Christian message as it is of any other. Indeed, Jesus described himself as the way, which is perhaps the most profound example of the medium being the message that there ever was! Messages are thus about more than just their content. To grasp the entire message, we need to know the source of the message and be aware of the messenger's intent.

Most of the commercial messages we hear come at us from mass media sources, and are intended to manipulate our behavior, whether we're aware that we're being manipulated or not. If you're curious, you can read Vance Packard's 1957 marketing classic *The Hidden Persuaders*, which describes the eight hidden motivators advertisers use to get us to buy things, by appealing subliminally to the instinctual desires and fears of the ego. It isn't pretty.

In contrast, messages about love are always gentle invitations, with no hint of coercion or manipulation. The source, wrote the famous Jesuit theologian Karl Rahner, is always God, but you and I are, among other things, the voice of God. You and I are the medium God has chosen to deliver God's messages of love. Each of us is some part of the experience of God of everyone that we've ever met. Study, worship and prayer certainly help tune up that package and our ability to deliver it, but the capability God gave us to be his voice has its origin deep within the loving and creative relationship God has with each and every one of us.

Let me tell you a little story. Several years ago, a group of us were sitting around my friend Ernie's fire pit after a really good barbecue. As we enjoyed each other's company in the warmth of the fire against the coolness of the evening, the experience of hearing the Good Shepherd's voice came up. We all agreed that it was pretty easy to hear the voice of God in our mutual friendship that evening, but our friend Sean said, "I think it goes deeper than that."

We asked him to explain, and he told us: "I remember when my son Tommy was coming into the world. Cindy and I used to talk and sing to 'The Lump,' as we called him before he was born.

---

3 Marshall McLuhan, *Understanding Media: The Extensions of Man* (New York: McGraw Hill, 1964).

I thought it was silly, but Cindy used to ask, 'How do you know whether he can hear or not?'"

"Anyway, when he was born, they wiped him off, wrapped him up in a blanket and handed him to me, screaming bloody murder and eyebrows at the vertical. Nobody told me what I was supposed to do, so I just put my face up right next to his, gave him a kiss and began singing 'Happy Birthday' to him. They say babies can't see much, but he gave me the longest stare anyone has ever given me and then stopped crying, as if I'd turned off a switch."

"He was as tiny and light as a bird, but I could feel him relax in my arms, and his eyebrows returned to normal. It hit me then that he knew who I was and that he was safe. I was his and he was mine and that was all that mattered. It was like the way it is sometimes after receiving Communion. Cindy and I think that somehow as I sang to him, he recognized my voice from the time before he was born."

"For me, hearing God's voice is like that. It feels like I'm recalling being loved from the time before I was even born. Tonight, with all of us together like this, I can feel God speaking to me through you, just like that." We all got kind of quiet just then, and we all knew what Sean said was true. In the warmth of our little circle of love, we knew we were each syllables being uttered from the mouth of God to one another.

Amid all the clutter of messages that assault us today, you and I can reliably pick out the ones that resonate with the sound of the voice of the Good Shepherd. They're the messages that are saturated with the love God has had for each and every one of us from all eternity. They're the messages that are intended only to invite us gently into deeper, increasingly more trusting relationship with him, without coercion or manipulation. They are the messages of love.

Questions For Discussion

1. Can you recall a time when God presented God's self to you though another person? What was that experience like?
2. What is your message to the world? From whence does the message come? Do you feel compelled to express it?

Forgiving Enemies

Who's your worst enemy? The topic comes up from time to time in gatherings at our place. Some say they have no enemies. Others ask for more time to work on the list. Many just mention the usual suspects: ISIS or the Communists. When it's my turn I quote Walt Kelly's Pogo and say, "We've found the enemy, and it's us." Love of enemies is rarely mentioned in these conversations.

Today's readings describe one of the tougher parts of being a follower of Jesus. If you feel uneasy when you hear these readings, you're not alone. That said, historians are certain that Jesus actually did tell us to love our enemies so, if we want to follow Jesus, loving enemies is not negotiable. That, however, mightn't mean what we think it means. Let's see.

A moment's glance at the crucifix tells us that Jesus walked the talk when it came to loving enemies. Jesus offers in himself, even to his worst enemies, the connection between humankind and the divine, regardless of whether or not we choose to accept the invitation. Saint Paul, in his letter to the Ephesians, characterizes what Jesus is doing as the breakdown of the enmity that existed, by our choice, between humans and God.

In receiving the Eucharist then, you and I are asked to pass along that invitation to connect with the divine, even to our worst enemies, offering love and being open to the love of others as best we can. The crucifix shows graphically what might be in store for those who choose to follow Jesus like this. It's no wonder that some hold back.

Adding to the discomfort we may feel about loving enemies is the sense the readings give us that Jesus didn't seem to take self-preservation seriously. He actually did, but he saw it differently than you or I might. Like Abishai in the first reading, our reaction to Saul's vulnerability would probably also have been to take advantage of it and kill him. He was the enemy, and we have to take care of ourselves, right? But like Jesus later, David saw it differently. He rejected Abishai's offer, entrusting his self-preservation to God alone. Although Saul may have chosen to make David his enemy, David didn't have to make Saul his.

This leads us to ask — who makes our enemies, anyway? Let me tell you a story. I meet with the people of Calix from time to time. Calix is a group of Catholic folks who struggle with alcohol addiction. As it turns out, alcohol abuse is a very effective way to make enemies.

We were talking about that not too long ago. By their own admission, much of what had been lovely and good in their lives had been destroyed by the selfishness and dishonesty that lay behind their addictive behavior. Loved ones had turned into enemies. At one point, I gently paraphrased the gospel passage we heard just a moment ago and asked them how it felt to hear Jesus speak like that. It got quiet for a few moments, but then one of the folks said, "Of course we should love our enemies — they're ours, we made them."

I pondered that phrase long after the meeting ended. Sure, there are groups of people in the world who'll never see things our way, but my friend hadn't been talking about our pre-packaged enemies like ISIS and the Communists. He was talking about enemies we'd made all by ourselves. The command to love our enemies challenges us to accept our own share of responsibility for the enmity that arose and undo the damage as best we can.

There's something deeper though, that lies at the heart of our need for redemption and suggests to us the most important reason we need to love our enemies. From time to time, I give talks to people young and old, and if the situation lends itself for me to do so I'll ask by a show of hands, "How many of you love yourself?" Most of the time, most of the hands, if not all, stay down. To me, that's so sad.

The word "enemy" comes from the Latin word *inimicus* which simply means "not a friend"... someone who doesn't love you. I asked earlier who your worst enemy was. Maybe Walt Kelly's Pogo had it right. For the folks in these audiences, and perhaps many here as well, our own worst enemy may be ourselves.

But if God loves us, why would we choose not to love ourselves? Loving ourselves as God does isn't about narcissism or egocentricity. It's about being a friend to ourselves; holding ourselves in high regard and always doing the best, most loving thing as our lives unfold; forgiving and asking forgiveness when things go awry. If we sense that we've somehow made ourselves our own worst enemy, then the call to love our enemies cannot be more urgent. Is it time perhaps to forgive our worst enemy, ourselves, for all the inelegance that comes with simply being human?

Maybe it's even more serious. The often-excruciating suffering I see at the hospital from time to time makes me wonder if, for some people, God is their worst enemy. "How can a good God let this happen to my child?", "Where was God when I needed God, anyway?" people often say to me angrily through clenched teeth.

In the moment, outbursts like these are perfectly understandable. It's simply how we deal with the strong emotions surrounding staggering losses and trauma. Later, when it's appropriate, I'll suggest to people that they consider forgiving God for making life hard the way it is, bitterly so at times, and perhaps even for making us as imperfect as we are.

Let me be clear: God doesn't need our forgiveness, but we benefit from doing the forgiving. Through it, we can embrace and ultimately come to accept the stark reality of what it means to be fully human, with all its joy and sadness, its goodness and its evil. In the end, as Saint Paul wrote, God is no one's enemy; never has been. It's actually quite the opposite. Examine a crucifix.

The deep meaning of the cross and resurrection becomes increasingly clear as we travel along this path of love and forgiveness. There is no harder work in life, nor any as rewarding or frankly, as crucial. Through it we can begin to accept ourselves, others and God with realistic compassion. In a word, we can begin to love our enemies.

Questions For Discussion

1. Who's your worst enemy?
2. What does forgiveness mean to you? To others? To God?
3. Why might forgiveness be connected somehow to self-acceptance?

Abuse

Let me tell you about a conversation I had with a man and his wife one night not too long ago, while serving as a chaplain over at the hospital. The man described himself as a former Catholic, disgusted at what he had been hearing about the crimes against children, the inexcusable cover-ups and what he felt was the general corruption of the Catholic church. His wife was equally indignant.

"How can you still be a Catholic?" he demanded of me, full of righteous indignation. "In good conscience I can't justify associating with people like you anymore. What kind of games do you play in your mind that allows you to stay?"

"You sound angry," I observed.

"You bet I'm angry," he replied. "I feel betrayed by people who ought to have known better. They took advantage of the most vulnerable of us all and made a mockery of the faith. How can so-called 'holy people' abuse innocent children like that? How can all the others cover it up?! I don't want to have anything to do with anyone like that anymore and you shouldn't either, if you had any courage."

"Suppose I was to tell you that members of my own family had been sexually abused," I asked. It got very quiet all of a sudden, and both he and his wife fixed me with their eyes.

"Who?" he asked.

"Me," I replied. "And another relative as well."

They were at a loss for words, so I continued. "In my case, the perpetrator was a family member. In the other it was a teacher. The only clergy involved were those who helped us come to grips with what had happened and offered us ways we could use to begin to reframe our lives. Far from abandoning our faith, we've gripped it the way you'd cling to a life preserver."

The man's wife looked at me and just said "I'm so sorry." I gave that statement the attention it deserves and went on.

"The perpetrators were never held accountable. One, we think, met an untimely end at his own hands, and the other is not in a position to be a problem to anyone anymore. But let me ask you a question, not to excuse the church or deflect attention from anything. If it's teachers who can be abusers, should we then never send our children to school? If it's family members who could turn out to be the problem, should we all then have nothing to do with our families? Tell me what you think."

They had nothing to offer, so I went on. "An abused person has had something stolen from him or her that can never be fully recovered. No amount of money, not even the billions the Catholic church has, for its own part, spent on abuse settlements so far, can ever restore what was taken from us."

"Some parts of our lives will always be painted in subdued colors, where for you the colors will always be bright and happy. The relationships we do manage to form will always be crippled by the ugliness we suffered earlier. Intimacy, if it comes at all, will be purchased at a price you probably cannot even begin to imagine. I do not know how I would have survived at all without the love of God and the support of those who share my faith. Some of us, as you well know, don't."

"We didn't know," the man said quietly. "We didn't mean to hurt you."

"You didn't," I replied honestly, "there is a part of all of us, our deepest identity, that belongs entirely to God. It's the place where God lives within us, so to speak. It's my deepest me, and it's untouchable by sin and illusion, beyond the reach of depravity, fantasy and the brutality of any human ego, including my own."[4]

"No, you cannot hurt my deepest me. But when I heard your anger, I knew I had to respond to it directly, in a way that might help you let go of it. Although you cannot hurt my deepest me, you can easily hurt yourself with your anger. Please believe me — I know that from my own bitter experience. When Jesus spoke of gouging out eyes and cutting off hands — all he meant is that if there's something about us that isn't loving or life giving, we need to get rid of it — not let it be part of us anymore. Anger is like that."

"It's not just the sex abuse that makes me angry," the man told me. "I experienced so many other instances of arrogance and disdain from so-called 'religious people.' Maybe your 'deepest me' hasn't been hurt, but I feel mine has."

[4] Thomas Merton, *Conjectures of a Guilty Bystander* (New York: Doubleday Religion, 1966), 182.

"You're probably not alone," I admitted, "but let me share some wisdom from Max Lucado, a wise pastor from another Christian tradition, who said a while back: 'Although I can't say what your past looked like, I can tell you with precision what your future's going to look like if you don't come to terms with your anger.'[5] Why let disappointment in other people's behavior cause you to turn away from the God who loves you, lives within you and sustains your being? It was Saint Augustine who remarked that God has many the church doesn't have, and the church has many that God doesn't have."

"It'll always be a mix but let me invite you to return to the Eucharist anyway," I urged them. I pointed to the crucifix in his room and remarked that if Jesus could forgive those who killed him, so was I called to forgive those who had killed a part of me. So was my relative and so was everyone else, including them."

"I'll forgive them when I see them all roasting in hell," the man said.

"Problem is," I replied, "you'd have to be there with them to see it, and that's a barbecue to which you probably wouldn't enjoy being invited."

His wife laughed as I said that and the mood in the room lightened up a bit. We went on to discuss other topics, and I left having received a promise from both of them that they'd give the church another try. "Something tells me you're probably right about the Eucharist, but we'll see," were the man's last words to me.

I hope they follow up on their promise. Life can indeed be brutal beyond comprehension, but the love of God goes far deeper than any evil of mankind can reach, and it's a love that can never be extinguished.

---

5   Max Lucado

Questions For Discussion

1. Everyone likely suffers abuse of some sort or another in life. Why might one person abuse another?
2. Why might an abuser seek to hide? Why might an abused person also seek to hide?
3. What is an appropriate response to abuse? To the abused? To the abuser?
4. Can abused people be healed? If so, how?

Joy And Happiness

In everyday speech, joy and happiness are frequently used synonymously, but I'd like to suggest to you that even though there's some overlap at the emotional level, there's actually a significant difference. Happiness can be a mile wide and an inch deep sometimes. Joy, though, goes down to the bone, and beyond. It's much more than just an emotion or simple Christmas card sentiment. Joy "animates our lives and ultimately leads to a life of satisfaction and meaning."[6]

Happiness generally reflects pleasure, but joy comes from grasping that our deepest needs and hopes are being met; it's unmistakable confirmation of our deepest worth. Anything from finding a parking space to our favorite team winning can bring us happiness, but joy comes to us in direct, exquisite encounters with the love of Jesus Christ, frequently as God comes to us disguised as other people. Happiness comes and goes and might even accompany joy for a bit. But true joy doesn't need the glee that goes along with happiness, and it lasts forever. Let me tell you a couple of stories and you can decide if you agree.

If you watched any of President Bush's funeral, you might have gotten a glimpse of how joy can emerge even in the unhappiest of moments. At one point during his eulogy, George W. said of his dad "As he aged, he taught us how to grow old with dignity, humor, and kindness — and, when the good Lord finally called, how to meet him with courage and with joy in the promise of what lies ahead."[7] For those who take Jesus Christ seriously, it would seem that even the sadness of death and separation doesn't eclipse the joy our faith promises. The good news of love never grows old.

Such an observation doesn't require anyone to die, either. Several years ago, while I was visiting patients over at the hospital, I encountered an older man and his wife waiting for the discharge staff to come and clear him for departure. They were obviously happy to be going home together and I asked about that. They

---

6 Desmond Tutu & the Dalai Lama, *The Book of Joy* (New York: Penguin, 2016),
7 https://www.thehindu.com/news/international/george-hw-bush-state-funeral-text-of-george-w-bushseulogy/article25675279.ece, December 6, 2018

told me that they'd been married for 68 years. I told them they'd been married longer than I'd been alive!

We laughed together and then they told me their story. High school sweethearts, he'd spent time in the Navy, rather like President Bush, while she had worked and carefully built up a nest egg for them. They married shortly after his discharge and together raised a large, happy, loving family. I asked what it felt like to have been married for 68 years and the husband said "Well, like everyone else I guess, we've had our ups and downs, triumphs and tragedies."

He paused for a moment and exchanged glances with his wife. Wordlessly, I could see them reading the story of their lives in each other's gaze. "We might not always have been what people nowadays would call 'happy'," he said, "but there was never a moment without joy; when you both have what your hearts most desire, you feel known, completely welcome, loved, safe and strong."

Pausing to hug his wife, he asked me if I was a theist and I said, yes, I believed in God. Then he told me, "What we wanted most was each other, and we got that. What surprised us after we'd been married for a while was that we actually wanted more; we both wanted to love and be loved as God loves us. In loving each other we found that God was the real source and object of our deepest love, our deepest joy. Maybe that's what Jesus meant when he referred to himself as 'The Way'."

I left the room in awe, dazzled by love like that. Our church teaches that to be saved is to enter into the joyful love of the Holy Trinity itself. To me, it seemed that these two lovely people already had one foot in that door.

Last story: A few of us VFW sorts were chatting over lunch one day about which military YouTube videos had stuck with us. I told them that one of my favorites was about a young Marine back from deployment in Afghanistan. His wife had arranged for him to surprise their two youngsters at school upon his return.

The clip had shown the children's reaction to seeing their dad. You can't watch any of these kinds of clips without getting a lump in your throat. The one thing the children had been hoping for, the one thing they wanted more than anything else was to have their dad back, and there he was — for real — right in front of them. It could so easily have been otherwise, but it wasn't.

I've never seen people hug one another as tightly as those two little people clung to their dad and he gripped them with that big bear hug men give to those they love. They all laughed and cried without restraint. "We were beyond happy," the Marine had said later, surrounded by his wife and children, "I don't know what the word is to describe a moment like that, and the moment hasn't really stopped. Somehow, it's for keeps. I wonder if heaven's like this."

That's joy. The elderly couple at the hospital know all about it, and George W. recognized it at his father's passing, too. Is it heaven? Maybe they all just had one foot in the door, but it's like that with the promised salvation we anticipate during Advent. Maybe life could be otherwise, but it's not. Enter deeply into the Eucharist now and see for yourself — joy and the love of God are real, right in front of us, right now and for keeps, just quietly awaiting your embrace and mine.

Questions For Discussion

1. What are "joy" and "happiness" to you? Can you give examples?
2. When have you been overwhelmed with joy?
3. Sometimes we want to cling to moments of happiness, as many a pop song relates. There are no handles on joy to which we can cling — it's simply there. Can you find situations in your life where the transitory nature of happiness was poignantly apparent, or the deep joy of being loved emerged into your conscious attention? How did those experiences make you feel?

Servant Leadership

Many years ago, I got some insight into what servant leadership might look like through a poem by Lao Tzu that went like this:

A leader is best when people barely know that he exists, not so good when people obey and acclaim him, worst when they despise him. Fail to honor people [and they will] fail to honor you. But of a good leader, who talks little, when his work is done, his aims fulfilled, they will all say, "We did this ourselves." [8]

Not much prestige at work there, I think you'd agree, and the only power we see operating is the power of many people's energy directed to accomplishing a goal they've been convinced is worth achieving. The poem illustrates Jesus' point that the best motivation for leadership and the exercise of power is not prestige and domination, but the service of love.

Some time ago, a group of us were chatting about memorable bosses we'd had over the years, both good and bad.

"I remember working for this one woman we all used to call Attila the Hen," my friend Ernie told me. "She was the kind of person for whom anyone's very best never seemed to be good enough. It wouldn't have been so bad if she hadn't been a screamer, too, and sarcastic. It was all about how good she looked, not us. I don't know how she got to where she'd gotten, but after just a few weeks on the job I knew I had to leave."

Our buddy Steve nodded with understanding and told us about a boss who had a quote from Niccolo Macchiavelli hanging in his office that read 'It is better to be feared than to be loved.' "I don't think he ever physically poisoned anyone," Steve said, "but you could get pretty sick just watching him operate behind other people's backs. I didn't stay there very long myself."

When it was our friend Kevin's turn, he said he'd decided to share a different kind of story. "When I first started out in computers," he told us, "all there was were mainframes — big bulky, complicated, and poorly documented. Most of us had to learn everything on the job."

---

8   https://aboutleaders.com/leaders-honor-thy-people/#gs.3v0tqo, March 31, 2019

"My first boss was a man by the name of Gene. He was a very likable person — tremendously encouraging, with deep faith and what we'd call an 'interesting' sense of humor. We hit it off immediately. I told him that I was pretty new to all this and would be grateful for all the help I could get. Gene liked that and told me "I'm going to help you become the best systems guy you can be. Sometimes I'm going to throw you in over your head, but all you ever have to do is ask for help though, and I'll be there for you."

Then he said something I'll never forget: "Don't think of me as your boss," Gene told me. "In fact, I don't want you to be intimidated by my experience or title either, so from here on in," he said with a wink, "just call out for your 'Slave' when you need me. We'll both know what you mean." We laughed together at that, and I told him it sounded pretty disrespectful, but he insisted, telling me with a grin that he was making me promise to do that because he thought it would take care of some other problems he had to deal with, too."

"When we first started, the rest of the staff was taken aback by me calling Gene my "Slave." Then they found it funny. Then I noticed them quietly begin to examine some of their own behaviors. A couple of guys who'd imagined themselves to be legends in their own minds and better than everyone else began to back off their angrily superior, dismissive attitudes and actually began to answer questions politely and become helpful to us new folks. If Gene could be a slave, they could be slaves, too. Maybe even better slaves."

"A few of the other newbies started to ask them about the way things worked, got good answers, and began to hope that they, too, could get confident at this job. A community was beginning to form in the unit where before there had been division, fear and isolation. It dawned on me one day what those other problems Gene had to deal with had been. He'd solved them by becoming 'the Slave.'"

"So it went for almost two years, as we developed our sea legs together under the guidance of a master technician and a fabulous leader. Gentle when he needed to be gentle, direct when there was call for that, but always 'the Slave,' not only to me, but to all of us, whenever anyone, even the geniuses, needed help. Consciously or unconsciously we all became each other's slaves, each in his or her own way."

"The day came when Gene didn't show up for work. It emerged that Gene had suffered a sudden, massive heart attack and died on his way to work. The letter from Gene's widow came to us later that month. She told us Gene had been so proud and grateful of the way our group had come together. We were, she told us, his most significant achievement."

"Being a religious guy, Gene had told his wife he led our group the way he thought Jesus would lead it, and they'd laughed together over his nickname, "the Slave." Her letter ended on a serious note though. He'd told his wife that if he ever died on his way to work or somewhere else, to make sure that someone told his people that he loved them. She'd promised to do so, and so she had. Our leader, 'the Slave,' had loved us, just as he had been loved by Jesus and asked to love those he led."

Every one of us is at various times in life a leader. What kind of leaders are we? Who are we more inclined to follow — Jesus or Machiavelli? Are we leading each other deeper into the fullness of the community of God's love, or have we chosen a different path?

Questions For Discussion

1. Would you describe yourself as a leader? If so, what is your definition of leadership? What would you say about the differences, if any, between Lao Tzu's concept, Jesus' and Machiavelli's?

2. What kind of leader are you most likely to follow?

3. Go to Google Translate, type in "command," and translate it from English to Greek. Now translate the word "instruct" and do likewise. Would you rather be commanded or instructed by God? By others? Might your response change anything about how you appropriate scripture?

Wisdom

The first steps in acquiring wisdom of any kind, secular or religious, are to receive it, then to understand it, then to make it your own and then to share it by the way we live. Wisdom is found both in scripture and the Eucharist. Each in its own way provides us with wisdom, one through words and the other through the direct experience of a life of love lived jointly with God; a life lived in awareness of the real presence of God.

Appropriating God's wisdom — making it our own, making it the foundation of who we are and how we behave, requires deliberate effort. I'd suggest to you that there's nothing like memorization to make wisdom part of who we are and how we operate. I remember vividly the first time I read the words of St. Paul to the Ephesians. They struck me as being so wise and so powerful that I simply had to make it part of who I was and how I operated. So, I memorized it. Here's the whole thing, acapella, from Saint Paul's letter to the Ephesians (4:29):

> *Never let evil talk pass your lips. Say only the good things people need to hear, things that will may impart grace to those who hear, and really help them. Do nothing to sadden the Holy Spirit with whom you were sealed against the day of redemption. Get rid of all passion and anger, all harsh words, slander and malice of every kind. In place of these, treat one another with kindness, compassion and mutual forgiveness, just as you have been forgiven in Christ.*[9]

It's part of me now, and it has come in handy for me and some of my friends who've decided they wanted to memorize it too.

Let me tell you a little story. I was chatting with my friend Ernie, who has those two teenagers I've mentioned to you in the past. He came home from a particularly tough situation at work one day, where he'd had to discipline a couple of people on his staff who were going after each other's throats. Little did he know he was going to encounter the same thing at the dinner table.

As his wife served dinner, his daughter, Alice, lit into one of her classmates.

---

9 Liturgy of the Hours version, modified for inclusive language and clarity by the author.

"Do you know what Rachel did today?" she asked her dad through glowering eyes.

"It wasn't on the news as I drove home," Ernie said, "why don't you tell me."

"That miserable excuse for a human being is telling people that I stole her boyfriend and made him hate her. It's not true! People like that shouldn't even exist. What a waste of food and air! He dumped her because she acts like a test pilot in a broom factory, that's what! She's as dumb as three rocks at the bottom of the sea, but at least he could figure that out!"

Ernie, having survived a very similar situation just hours earlier, looked at Alice with calm empathy and remarked: "You seem upset."

"Upset? You bet I'm upset," Alice roared. "I am personally going to kill that disgusting…"

Ernie interrupted her as his wife grasped Alice's arm, since you don't want to be waving an arm that's holding a steak knife. "Alice," Ernie said calmly, "I just had a situation at work today exactly like what you're describing."

"Did you kill anybody?" Alice asked.

"No," Ernie replied. "Would you like to know what I did?"

"Sure," Alice said, still shaking with anger. "One of my men came into my office furious at his co-worker, yelling and calling him names. I knew he was a parishioner, like us, so I told him to sit down. Then I took the little crucifix you gave me for my birthday last year, that I keep on the credenza in my office, and placed it in front of him. He got very quiet, very quickly."

Ernie's wife got up and silently put the crucifix they keep in the kitchen on the dinner table as Ernie continued.

"We talked rationally from then on and yes, there had been an injustice which will be corrected. The evil talk though? I told him it had to stop. It's one thing to be an observer of our angry thoughts and strong emotions, and quite another to be a victim of them. I asked him to look at the crucifix and tell me what Jesus did to the people who were spreading lies about him and arranging for him to be killed. Do you know what Jesus did, Alice?"

"He should've sent them all to hell," Alice snarled.

"Well, he didn't," Ernie said. "Jesus forgave them because they really didn't know what they were doing. In doing so, he showed us what anyone who wants to be like him should do."

"Are you telling me I have to forgive that…that…" Alice stuttered.

"Sooner or later," Ernie nodded. "Why let a person who upsets you live rent-free in your brain, Alice? And you certainly don't want to retaliate in kind, either. Remember that line from Saint Paul I use all the time? 'Never let evil talk pass your lips. Say only the good things people need to hear — things that will really help them….' Try it. To paraphrase Mark Twain, you will astonish those who don't like you and surprise those who expect you to retaliate in kind."

"You will also be creating an opportunity for both of you to discover some important things about yourselves — some deep goodness that never requires cutting other people down and spreading lies about them. It's part of growing up, Alice," Ernie said. "Try it and let me know what happens."

"Did it work for you?" Alice wanted to know.

"I can't tell for sure just yet," Ernie replied honestly, "but he did ask to borrow my crucifix. Draw strength from the living wisdom of God's presence, Alice, and invite God to become visible to others through you. Wisdom expressed is love unleashed, and the Lord knows how badly you, Rachel, and our whole world needs that today."

Questions For Discussion

1. Consider your speech this week in the light of that quote from Ephesians. Do you see any room for improvement?
2. What is the difference between having an opinion about someone and gossip?
3. It's often a good idea to "look over the shoulder" of our speech to see what motivated it.

The Good Shepherd

My friend, Bob Blair, who's also a deacon, worked for many years on a farm not too far from here, so I asked him what he thought it meant to be a Good Shepherd these days. He laughed and told me he had a story he thought I'd enjoy.

One day, when he was driving a tractor out to the north forty somewhere, he noticed a strange looking dark lump on the ground off to the left. Curious, he turned the tractor and went to investigate. He found a newborn calf lying on the ground, still wet from birth. Its mother was nowhere to be found. The calf had been born and abandoned.

Bob knew how stories like that ended and what he had to do next. Turning off the tractor, he went over to the calf, picked it up and slung it over his shoulders. If he could get the calf to safety, he knew it would have a chance at life in spite of having been abandoned by its mom.

As he walked back to the barn, the calf, having no idea of what was happening to it, mooed unhappily and squirmed around, trying to get away. Bob spoke to it in that calm, consoling voice all deacons have. The calf didn't understand English though and Bob quickly found himself covered with a smelly cocktail of materials that until very recently had been inside the calf.

The complexion of Bob's words to the calf changed dramatically, but he soon fell quiet again as he realized that the calf had no idea what was happening to it and was just scared out of its wits. In his heart he knew that he was all that stood between the calf and certain death. No matter what, there was no way he was going to let that calf down.

Eventually he got the calf back to the barn, where he was greeted by the farmer with surprise, laughter, and gratitude. Bob started to laugh too, in spite of being a mess. What difference did it make what he looked and smelled like, anyway? The calf had been saved.

Laughing together, they called Bob's wife, Elaine, who brought him some clean clothes and shared in the joy. After a shower and a change of clothes the farmer warmly thanked Bob again and told him: "You're what it means to be a Good Shepherd." Bob was too humble to share the spotlight with Jesus, so he said he was just happy that God had used him to save the life of that helpless little calf.

Some of the parallels between Bob's experience and the parable of the Good Shepherd are pretty obvious, but others are perhaps not. Let's take a look. At the simplest level we could ask ourselves if we're the kind of people who would stop to save a helpless animal from certain death. Would we drop what we're doing and go help, or would we prefer to think that it's not our job? I suspect most of us would stop and help, if we were confident we weren't going to make matters worse or get hurt. But what about stopping to help people we encounter who are leading lives headed toward certain death? What might we choose to do?

Let's go beyond the obvious now and take a look at things from the calf's perspective, since it's really our human perspective, too. Like the abandoned calf, here we are on earth, pretty helpless, doomed to death unless a Good Shepherd comes along to save us. Are we receptive to God's intervention through Jesus, or do we sometimes find ourselves more like Bob's calf, bleating and making a big mess?

If we dwell on that question for a while, we'll soon find ourselves pondering the limitations of human understanding and the radical helplessness that's implicit in the human condition. Bob's little calf had no idea of what its situation was, how much trouble it was in, or what this person carrying it was up to. Although we know that Bob was doing the kind and compassionate thing for the calf, the calf had no such understanding. All it knew was that it was being taken someplace it couldn't imagine, and that it was absolutely not in control.

Are there perhaps times in our lives when we too are challenged to trust without understanding? Do we find ourselves responding to lack of control like the calf, dumping on the very people trying to save us?

My friend Roger told me about a time in his life like that. In a two-week period, he lost his job, he and his wife suffered the miscarriage of their firstborn twins, and his beloved dad told him he had just been diagnosed with pancreatic cancer. If you ever wanted to see what an angry, helpless person looked like, you'd have seen him sitting there in Starbuck's that rainy morning.

He was furious with God and told me he felt picked out for special punishment even though no one had done anything to deserve it. He didn't understand and challenged me to explain.

After sincerely extending my condolences, I told him I didn't run the universe and had no rationale to give him beyond pointing out that everything, enormously sad as it had been, had also been in the realm of things that can befall anyone, anywhere. I reminded him that I taught statistics over at RPI and that although he might've felt singled out, in reality he was no exception.

Since he was a man of faith, I told him, all he could realistically do was to lean into his relationship with God, embrace the Eucharist, pray for the grace of trust in the absence of understanding, and face what had happened to him as best he could with his family and friends. Perhaps in time he might be in a position to reflect and find some hidden wisdom in the events that had befallen him, appreciate the Eucharist from an entirely new perspective, and maybe eventually provide consolation to others going through what he himself had experienced.

If he was like me, I said, he might just find it's sometimes the case that the deepest wisdom and fullness of life comes by way of life's most bitter suffering. How often I had been angrily helpless in my life, I told my friend, only to find myself rescued by God and taken to a place I could never have imagined. It all went better when I had the presence of mind to allow God to carry me; to trust without understanding.

Sure, it's okay in the moment for us to roar at life's tribulations, I told him, but it's also wise to remember as best we can while we're doing so that we're all being carried on the shoulders of the best shepherd humanity has ever known, and that there's no way he's ever going to let any of us down, no matter what.

Questions For Discussion

1. Describe a "calf" you have rescued or wish you could have rescued in life?
2. Have you ever been the calf? Describe the experience in loving, self-compassionate detail.
3. How do you respond when God seems to single you out for special, unwanted attention?
4. How do you cope?
5. How does your response make you feel?

Exorcism

Do you remember your last exorcism? For most of us, it was probably at our baptism, when the priest or deacon intoned the words:

"Almighty and ever-living God, you sent your only Son into the world to cast out the power of Satan, spirit of evil, to rescue man from the kingdom of darkness, and bring him into the splendor of your kingdom of light. We pray for these children: set them free from original sin, make them temples of your glory, and send your Holy Spirit to dwell with them. We ask this through Christ our Lord."[10]

Any prayer of exorcism is simply a prayer that the church offers asking God to free people from evil persons, places and circumstances. In the case of baptism, we ask God not so much to free, but to protect those being baptized from evil, and release them from the effects of original sin — that human inclination we all have to choose our own way rather than God's, roll off the table and shatter on the floor.

This little exorcism prayer also sums up the mission of Jesus as it's expressed in the gospel and makes that part of his mission very personal for each of us. As the gospel passage clearly illustrates, Jesus makes the dominion of God present and active. Placing ourselves in God's hands through prayer and frequent reception of the Eucharist allows Jesus to act through us too, making the dominion of God present and active in our own lives, full of the life and love God wills us to enjoy.

My friend Dave has two daughters in their twenties now. Sally is a wonderful and talented young woman with a delightful personality. She's a lot smarter than I am and is on track to become a physician, specializing in emergency care. Dave is awfully proud of her. Vicky is another story altogether.

"I think Vicky needs an exorcism, Tim," Dave told me one day over lunch, "Can you do that?"

I told him I would be vaporized by the archbishop if I tried to pull off a stunt like that, but I asked him why he thought Vicky needed an exorcism.

---

10 http://www.catholicliturgy.com/index.cfm/FuseAction/TextContents/Index/4/SubIndex/67/TextIndex/7. January 22, 2018

"Sally understands love and service," Dave said. "She and her friends volunteer their time to read to kids and visit folks in the hospital. They all go to mass together and share a pretty vivid prayer life. It's really nothing more than what we did at home when she was growing up. Vicky doesn't do any of that."

"Why do you think that is?" I asked.

"She has some friends I wish she didn't have," Dave explained. "She doesn't go to church with us, and I have no idea if she even has a prayer life anymore. When we invite her to join us, she comes back with 'What has your religion got to do with me? Are you trying to control my life?'"

I told him that sounded a lot like a gospel passage with which I was familiar, but the words didn't come from the mouth of anyone we'd care to be like.

"If you're thinking of the same passage I'm thinking of, then you understand why I think she needs an exorcism," Dave said.

I suggested he keep praying, loving his daughter and be open to God's action. If he really thought an exorcism was in order, he'd have to take it up with his pastor.

A few months later we were sharing lunch again and Dave was excited about some news he wanted to share with me. We unwrapped our sandwiches and he began.

"Vicky was at a party two weeks ago with some of those friends I wished she didn't have," Dave said. "They all got pretty drunk or worse. Then one of her closest friends, Rachel, fell to the floor, unconscious. That sobered everyone up in a big hurry. Someone called 911. Vicky noticed that her friends were scurrying to get rid of things they didn't want to be caught with. No one was paying attention to Rachel. Vicky did what she could, and the EMTs arrived quickly enough. She went with Rachel in the ambulance to the hospital, telling the EMTs what she knew of what had gone on."

"Was Sally on call in the Emergency Department that night?" I asked.

Dave smiled and said "That's what I wanted to tell you. Vicky watched as her sister and the rest of the team took care of Rachel. When they had her stabilized, Sally walked over to Vicky they hugged the kind of hug people who love one another give after a close brush with death.

Then she fixed her sister with a steely glare and said 'I hope it's not you I'll have to treat next time. When she wakes up, why don't you and Rachel go schedule an exorcism for yourselves. You don't seem to know what living a good life really means. Something evil's got a grip on you, Vicky, and you'd better get rid of it. Rachel's lucky — she'll live. Not everyone's that lucky."

Dave stopped, but there was still a little grin on his face.

"Awesome," I said. "I'll bet you're pretty proud of Sally — she sounds just like Jesus!"

"You bet I'm proud of her Tim," Dave said, "but not as much as I am as of Vicky. She's back in church again with us now. She's dropping her bad friends and is starting to follow her sister's lead to get back on the straight and narrow. That's hard work. Looks like all she needed was a good scare."

"A good scare," I replied, "or perhaps an exorcism by another name."

Questions For Discussion

1. Have you ever had a good scare that helped to set you straight? If so, describe it in loving, empathetic detail.
2. Can you write an "exorcism" prayer for someone you know? N.B., if you think you need a real exorcism, please contact your local pastor and diocesan ordinary.

Where Was God?

One of the folks I see down at the gym from time to time knows that I'm a deacon. He asked me just recently what I made of that terrible mass shooting in Las Vegas in which sixty people were killed and 413 were wounded. "Where was God in all that, anyway?" he wanted to know.

I replied that Saint Theresa of Avila had observed that there are many ways to be in a place. We can be someplace aware of being in God's presence and the guy right next to us can be totally unaware that God even exists. That night, I told him, God was with everyone but not everyone was with God.

Not satisfied, he asked: "How could a loving God allow something like that to happen?" I told him that our church teaches that absolute love is not possible without absolute freedom. That means we all continually have to make choices about love in our lives, and God does not dictate the outcome — ever, despite the risk of profound evil. We can choose to render to God what's God's and return that love or behave like the folks described in Psalm 81. "So I thrust them away to the hardness of their heart; 'Let them walk in their own machinations.'"

"If you want to know how that expression 'walk in their own machinations' plays out," I told him, "don't stop at last week's paper — read the history of the world and its bloodbaths. Choose not to return God's love and whoa — everybody duck!"

"Oh, and your Christianity would've prevented all that?" he sneered. "Your guess is as good as mine," I replied, "but I do agree with G.K. Chesterton that the problem with Christianity isn't that it has been tried and found wanting, but that it hasn't been tried,[11] certainly not by the troublemakers. Hitler was a baptized Catholic, but something inclines me to doubt that he practiced his faith with any degree of serious intent or regularity. I think we both know who his God really was."

"People like him aren't aware that they have to make any kind of decision about love," my friend argued. "Since they don't believe in God, there's no offer of love to return."

11 https://www.brainyquote.com/quotes/gilbert_k_chesterton_102389, February 8, 2020

"You've hit the nail on the head," I told him.

"I did?" he asked, astonished that we actually agreed about something,

"Sure — the fundamental problem is awareness," I said.

"No, it isn't," he replied, "it is belief."

"Awareness precedes belief though," I countered.

"Awareness of what?" he asked.

"For starters, awareness of being around," I told him. "My awareness that I exist is the stimulus for all those puzzling questions about who I am, where I am and what this is all about. Wrestling with those questions is what leads to belief, or unbelief. Believers come to find within themselves an urge to express thanks, praise and love. It's all that God asks us to render back."

"Sorry, Tim," he said, "No god made me — I'm a random event."

"No, you're not 'random,' you're a certainty," I told him. "You and I are enormously improbable but irrefutable certainties. Let me tell you: I used to teach graduate statistics at RPI. One day I told the students we were going to compute the probability of exactly them showing up. If you go back to your grandparents, given all the moving parts, the probability of exactly you showing up is one in several billion. When we took it all the way back to the trilobites in your family tree crawling around in the prehistoric ooze, your probability goes to roughly one in ten to the 400 thousandth power. Compared to your being around, winning the lottery is an absolute certainty, so don't give me this 'I'm random' line. Your existence is a fact. If anything, you're a miracle."

"There's no such thing as a miracle," he snorted. "Look in the mirror some time," I suggested. "All those trillions of exquisitely coordinated cells of you. Become aware that the distance between you and pure miracle is vanishingly small. Then, when you're done admiring yourself, take a look around you and see if you can detect any other miracles just like you!"

"I'll try that," he laughed. "I think you're nuts, Tim, but who knows?"

"If you really do try," I suggested, "just be grateful and give thanks. You don't even need to have an image of who it is that you're thanking. Just do it. It's the first step in the path towards the discovery of unconditional love. You might end up face-to-face with the surprise of your life."

"I'll let you know how it turns out," he said. I told him I'd be delighted to hear how it went and we went off to finish our workouts.

Questions For Discussion

1. What is the experience of being in the presence of God like for you? Consider physiological, spiritual, emotional, and intellectual dimensions for starters.
2. Describe an experience or two in your life you'd consider a miracle. What was the experience of the presence of God like for you in those moments?

It's Not Fair!

When our three children were little, every so often one of them would come to me or my wife and ask which of them was our favorite. Now, there are some questions in life which have only one correct answer. For example, when your wife asks you if her new dress makes her look fat, most men have come to realize one way or the other that "No, dear" is the only answer that will do.

Likewise, to our children's question, there's only one right answer: "We love you each exactly the same." As we came to find out, and maybe you have, too, that's not the question they were really asking nor the answer for which they were looking; it was something else. I was talking about this with my friend Ernie not too long ago. He agreed and told me that his daughter Alice had come to him just last week and accused him of loving her brother more than her.

"I asked her to tell me more," Ernie said, "and she told me: 'You love him more than me because he does the lawn, shovels the snow, washes the car without asking, hangs up all his clothes and does everything well in school.'"

"I told her that was all true, but we loved her just the same as him even though she didn't do some of those things. She wasn't buying a syllable of that, and I could see that it was pointless to try to convince her, so I told her 'Alice — I'm going to tell you a big secret right now that you can never share with anyone, under penalty of death.'"

"Alice loves secrets, especially sharing them with other people, so she listened up closely. Then I leaned toward her and whispered, 'Alice, you're actually my favorite — you always have been.'

I could tell that she had instantly stopped thinking about what she was planning to say next because her jaw dropped, and she asked me to repeat myself. I did and reminded her under penalty of death not to tell anyone, especially her brother."

"So, then she went right out and told him?" I asked Ernie.

"Of course," Ernie said, "and it wasn't five minutes later that Tommy came in and asked if he could have a word with me."

"That must have been fun," I remarked.

"Actually, it was," Ernie replied.

"What did you say?" I asked.

"I told him he was actually my favorite," Ernie said, "— always had been. You should've seen the expression on his face.

"'You can't have two favorites, Dad!' he told me."

"'Are you telling me it's not fair?' I asked."

"'No, it's not about being fair,'" Tommy told me, "'it's about being logical.'"

"I told him I agreed, but that he needed to learn a thing or two about the logic of love. Then I asked him to fetch his sister and join my wife and me at the kitchen table.

"'You're both my favorites,' I told them. 'Always have been. You're my favorite Alice and you're my favorite Tommy,' I explained."

"'I can't love either one of you more than I do, nor can mom. You both always have all our love, equally, no matter what you do or don't do. The logic of love is that there is no logic. There are no calculations or pay scales, and comparisons have no meaning.'"

"My wife elaborated, saying, 'It's like the way it is at church when we go up to receive Communion. No one gets *more* Jesus than anyone else. Love doesn't work that way. Everyone gets the same gift. It's God's way of saying that God loves us each of us exactly the same.'"

"'But doesn't God love some people more?'" Alice asked. "'I mean like saints and holy people?'"

"Frances and I shook our heads. 'No, Alice,' I explained, 'no saint would ever ask God to love her or him more than anyone else. If anything, like Saint Paul remarked once, they might wish it to be just the opposite if it would bring people closer to God. You see, saints know that there's a big problem with "more," I told her.'"

"'What's the problem?'" Alice asked."

"'Remember when we watched that old movie, *Wall Street*, on Netflix last summer?' I asked."

"'Not really,' Alice and Tommy replied."

"'Well, no matter,' I said, 'There was a wonderful line in it when one of the characters asked another, "What's enough for you, anyway?" He answered "More. More is enough for me."'"

"'That kind of "more,"' I told Alice, 'Never has enough, even though it has everything it needs.'"

47

"'Why are some people like that?' Tommy asked me."

"'I don't run the universe, Tommy,' I told him. 'Maybe for some it's greed, fear for others, envy perhaps. Whatever it is, it's not love. Love in a person always seeks what's good for others before it seeks what's good for itself. That's what "enough" means to love. It's always looking out for number one, and number one is always someone else.'"

"Tommy and Alice looked at each other and then at us," Ernie said.

"Then Alice told me quietly, 'You know, Dad, I think the question I was really asking was just whether or not you really loved me, not whether you loved Tommy more. Sometimes I feel afraid I have to earn your love, that somehow, I'm not enough, that I should be something more. But I hear you telling me love doesn't work that way.'"

"My wife and I shook our heads with a smile and gently touched our children's arms. 'No, Alice,' I said, 'it isn't that way with our love for you, and it certainly isn't that way with God's love for any of us.'"

"Alice and Tommy smiled back, relaxed, and Alice said, "Thanks for setting us straight. Love you guys!""

Questions For Discussion

1. When have you felt as if you were unlovable or not good enough? Describe those moments in loving, compassionate detail.

2. What do you imagine "fair" means to God?

3. Imagine for a moment what total, unconditional love and acceptance, freely and undeservedly given might feel like. How did that experience make you feel? Can you think of a reason why anyone would reject such an offer? What does your answer tell you about the difference between how you might be looking at yourself and the way God does?

4. Look at a crucifix now (not a cross). What might you see now that you didn't see before you considered the previous questions?

Transfiguration

This is one of the few homilies that appears in its entirety. The reason has to do with the picture you'll find at the end (no peeking!). It was taken by Mark Pickett during the mass at which I preached this homily. It is not photo-shopped. If you have trouble grasping your deepest identity, believing that there are *no* coincidences in life, and that your destiny and mine is simply jaw-dropping, the next few pages should cure you of all that.

How many people do you know, and how well do you think you really know them? Reading the scriptures and pondering what they might mean to us these days led me to wonder about that. I found that researchers at Columbia University have estimated that the average American knows somewhere around 611 people. It could be as low as 290 or so; a lot depends on your estimation strategy.

Take a moment and check your own inventory — who's there? Don't forget to count yourself. Then go ahead and add in your family, friends, acquaintances, co-workers, perhaps an enemy or two and, if you're really unlucky, the police, the FBI and the IRS.

Other research suggests that we know only 10 to 25 of those 611 people well enough to trust them.[12,13] Somewhere among our list of trusted people are our closest friends and family members — people who we trust would do anything for us, anytime. It is to these people alone that we feel comfortable revealing our deepest selves and the desires of our heart.

It may be that part of the reason Jesus chose only Peter, James and John to experience the vision of his deepest self was that he knew they were going to be the ones entrusted with the mission to carry the good news of God's merciful, compassionate love to the world after his death and resurrection.

In the end, these three disciples proved themselves to be indeed capable of bearing that trust, eventually becoming willing to

---

12 http://citeseerx.ist.psu.edu/viewdoc/download?-doi=10.1.1.485.9778&rep=rep1&type=pdf, July 15, 2017
13 Tyler McCormick, "How Many People Do You Know? Efficiently Estimating Personal Network Size," *Journal of the American Statistical Association* (March 2010).

do anything, anytime for Jesus, up to and including surrendering their lives. Peter led the church in its formative years and was martyred for his efforts. James did likewise, also giving his life. John, scripture tells us, was the disciple Jesus especially loved.

Like Peter, James and John, you and I have just now personally witnessed the Transfiguration, by way of the scriptures. That means that we, too, have been entrusted with exactly the same mission as Peter, James, and John, for exactly the same reason. Apparently, Jesus Christ considers you and me to be among those closest to his heart, those he can surely trust.

The questions that beg to be asked are: Can we say we're willing to do anything for God, anytime? Do we share our deepest selves and the desires of our heart with God? Is God first among those closest to our heart?

There's a deeper motivation for God's desire to number us among those closest to his heart than just being best friends. Paragraph 460 of our Catechism tell us what it is: "The Word became flesh to make us "partakers of the divine nature" ..."For the Son of God became man so that we might become God." That's your destiny and mine. The Transfiguration shows us the astonishing truth of what your deepest you and my deepest me actually looks like. Every so often we get a glimpse of who we really are, for there's a transfiguration event of some kind in everyone's life. If you haven't experienced one just yet, stay tuned.

My friend Ernie told me one day what his was like. He and his wife, Frances, have been married for about 37 years now. One day, when we were walking along the river over in Collinsville he told me the story. "Frances and I were working together in the garden," he said. "The sun was low in the sky, and she was over on the other side. I looked up and suddenly saw her lit from behind by the sun, outlined in luminous brilliance. It was like a vision — the light illuminated her like the glow of God's presence, and she seemed one with the light. I'd never seen her like that. You know how Saint Paul says we live and move and have our being in Christ? There it was, in real life, flashing for just an instant right in front of my eyes."

"I must've made an unusual noise, because the next thing she said was 'Ernie, are you okay?' I told her I thought I'd just seen her innermost being. She looked at me dubiously, raised her eyebrows, and told me not to tell anyone about it until after her resurrection. I touched her arm and said, 'No, seriously, I suddenly saw you just now in a way I never have before. It's as if I'd just seen for the very first time the deepest reality of the person I really love.'"

"That got her attention. We went inside and I told her more. I can't explain where any of it came from, except to say that everything that bubbled up from me was full of excitement, amazement, love and gratitude. We ended up in each other's arms, laughing with joy. Later on, she told me, 'I knew that you knew me and loved me, but you've never spoken to me like that. No one has. Maybe you really did see my deepest me out there in the garden. By the way, who do I look like the rest of the time?'"

Then Ernie turned to me and said: "I'm not telling you I had a vision or experienced some kind of miracle, but in that moment, I got to see something I needed to see. You don't think I'm nuts, do you?"

"Not at all," I replied. "Saint Catherine of Genoa used to tell everyone she met, 'my deepest me is God.' You actually might have been privileged to have seen in Frances something even more profound than what you thought you saw out there. The person you really love might just be God, alive and active with, within and all around Frances."

I tell you that story because yes, the Transfiguration is fundamentally about Jesus, his origin and mission. It was intended to give Peter, James, and John strength to deal with the pain of Jesus' passion, open their minds to understand his resurrection, and make them committed to remembering it all in their Eucharistic celebrations, just as we're doing right now.

It also shows you and me something we need to see if we're to claim that we really know ourselves, or anyone else for that matter. Turning the gem of the transfiguration of Jesus around in the light of God's love clearly shows that when Jesus revealed his deepest self to his closest disciples, he also revealed to us the deepest truth about you and me, our life right now and our ultimate destiny. Now he trusts us, equally his closest disciples, to do whatever it takes to carry that message of intense love and unimaginable intimacy to the world.

Okay, you can peek now. Remember the advice to "stay tuned?"

There's a passage from scripture that explains what's going on:

> "No longer will your teacher hide himself,
> but with your own eyes you shall see your teacher,
> And your ears shall hear a word behind you:
> 'This is the way; walk in it,'
> when you would turn to the right or the left." Isaiah 30:20-21

Spooky, eh?

Questions For Discussion

1. How well do you think you know yourself? Many folks find writing their own obituary a sobering experience. Give it a shot. How does it differ from a birth announcement?
2. In your opinion, are transfiguration and resurrection related in any way?
3. Have you ever glimpsed your inmost self? Another's self? If so, what was that experience like?

You Look Just Like Jesus

For several years I was a volunteer chaplain at a local hospital. From time to time, I'd do an overnight double-shift to give the staff chaplains a break. On occasion I'd walk into a patient's room in the middle of the night, and they'd wake up and be alarmed to see an old guy with a white beard approaching their bed. I'd reassure them that no, I wasn't God, and no, you're not dead. When they'd calmed down, we'd get on with business.

One evening I was called to spend some time with a woman who was scheduled for surgery the next day. She was quite apprehensive about what was going to happen to her, and anxious about the prospect of dying during the procedure. She was a Christian, and there were things on her mind.

In response to her questions, I told her I was there simply to listen — she could say anything she felt comfortable saying. If she wished, we could pray together, but I would follow her lead on that. Staring intently at me, she gripped my arm tightly and began to share her pain. She said she was deeply worried about some of the things she had done in her life. Frankly, she admitted, she hadn't thought that God and God's law of love were all that important for most of her life. She realized that she had been dazzled by money, power, and control, and now she was terrified by the prospect of God's judgment, as the real prospect of her death loomed before her.

No one's story is simple. The depth and extent of her pain, both received and inflicted, was staggering, and I began to feel enormously unworthy and incapable. With her permission, we prayed a little bit, and read some Psalms — 23 and 103 — if I recall correctly. In my heart, I prayed "Dear God — help — I have no idea how you want me to respond right now." God, I need to tell you, has never failed to respond to that prayer, sometimes in breathtaking ways.

In those next moments I felt like a spectator as God reached out through me to her, to reassure her of his merciful love, and allay her fears about his judgment. I felt as if someone else was doing the listening and talking; there was really no Tim there at all. Never in a million years would I have come up with those words and those gestures. I watched as her face and voice gradually relaxed and her grip on my arm loosened. Her doctor arrived eventually and was astonished to see her patient so much calmer and less anxious than she'd been just a short while ago. So was I.

I gently suggested some professional follow-up as I stood up to leave. With a smile, the patient thanked me and then asked, "Has anyone ever told you that you look like Jesus?"

I chuckled and told her about the patients who thought I was God and she laughed too, but then she said seriously, "No, it's not just your appearance. It's something more. Do you know what I mean?" Our eyes met and I nodded thanks to her wordlessly. "Believe me, lady," I thought to myself as I left the room, "I know exactly what you mean."

Questions For Discussion

1. Has anyone ever told you that you were like Jesus, or an angel, or a healing spirit to them?
2. What's it like to be like Jesus, do you think?
3. Can you describe a time when someone appeared to you either as Jesus or as an emissary from him?

Blindness

One day, young Patty went to her dad with a problem. There had been an argument in the lunchroom at school. One of her classmates was a fundamentalist in his religious tradition, and decided he needed to tell everyone who didn't believe what he believed; the way he believed it, that they were going to hell.

"I started to tell him I was a Catholic but he didn't even let me finish my sentence," Patty said. "I was definitely going to hell because we pray to Mary instead of God, call mere men 'Father' and listen to the pope instead of just the Bible."

"What did you and your friends do, Pat?" her dad asked.

"We just let him talk, Dad," Patty said. "I wanted to tell him we pray *with* Mary, not *to* her and are just being respectful and honoring our tradition and all that, but nobody could get a word in edgewise. He only wanted to see things his way."

"What a shame," Dad said. "If he's that kind of blind, he'll never get to know you, or maybe even anyone, more than superficially. I wonder if he'll ever really get to know God."

"He could spout Bible passages from memory," Patty said, "He sounds like he knows God pretty well."

"Perhaps he does," Dad said. "But I wonder how close that relationship really is. Knowing *about* God isn't the same thing as knowing God. If he won't listen to you to find out who you are, why would anyone think he's listening to God? You're an expression of God's love just like everyone else, but it seems he doesn't want to see that. Sounds like he thinks he knows it all. Did I ever tell you the story about Mr. O'Toole before he got married?"

"No," Patty said.

"Before he married Mrs. O'Toole, he had gone out with a woman who worked for the CIA."

"Wow — I didn't know that" Patty said. "How come they didn't get married?"

"O'Toole couldn't stand it, Pat," her dad said. "Every time they went on a date, she would tell him everything he'd done since their last date."

"Creepy, Dad," Patty exclaimed. "Your friend at school is like that, too," Dad continued. "Imagine yourself at a party where someone walks up to you without introducing himself and starts telling you who you are, without ever asking you anything about yourself."

"That would be weird, Dad," Patty said.

"And suppose when you tried to correct him, he angrily told you that you were wrong about yourself and told you to shut up."

"I'd call you, grab my coat and run, Dad," Patty said. "But nobody really does that, do they?"

"It's done all the time with God, Patty," Dad said. "Folks who've never introduced themselves to God start telling God what God's all about and prefer their own stories so much they decide that not only God, but the rest of us need to know too. Sometimes I think the worst form of blindness is to be only able to see things the way you happen to think they are."

"Are you saying my friend at school is like that, Dad?" Patty asked.

"I can't say — I don't know him," Dad admitted. "To know people, you have to listen to them, it seems to me, and listen deeply. Before I ventured an opinion about your friend at school, I'd want to invite him to introduce himself to me. Sort of the way we invite God to introduce himself to us when we pray intentionally."

"I've never invited God to introduce himself to me, Dad," Patty said. "People have just told me about God."

"That'll carry you for a while, Pat," Dad said, "But to grow up and to see God in more and more of God's lovely splendor, you have to issue that invitation, get some practice in being really quiet and attentive, and let God introduce himself in your life. I think you'll be pleasantly surprised, if not downright astonished, at how that introduction goes. God won't show up uninvited, and I'm sure you don't want to stay in the dark about God."

There's something about the human condition that renders us blind to ourselves, those around us, and God. But it needn't stay that way unless we deliberately want it to remain so. Perhaps on our Lenten journey we can open ourselves to experience God, our neighbor and our deepest self, and see it all as it really is. Then it will be no longer the blind leading who are leading the blind, but God.

Questions For Discussion

1. What are your relationships like with people of other faiths?
2. What is your relationship with Mary, if any?
3. Why do you think someone needs to present himself or herself as a know-it-all? Does your response lead you to be compassionate or perhaps something else?

Blessing

I used to volunteer at a local hospital as a friendly visitor. I'd get a list of folks and I would stop in and see if they were up for a visit. One day, I went into a room where a young man was lying in bed with a colostomy bag hanging by his side. His parents were there too. He was in pretty good spirits, but his parents weren't. I knew from my list they were Catholic, so I introduced myself as a Catholic deacon.

As the visit unfolded, we prayed a bit and I asked if they would like a blessing. That sent the parents over the top. They told me they were pretty steamed that God would allow their son to suffer the way he was. Pointing to the colostomy bag, the young man's dad growled at me: "I suppose to you this is some kind of blessing."

I recalled in the moment something I'd read in Pope John Paul II's encyclical about suffering[14] and said "I don't think I'd put it that way. But sooner or later," I continued, "after your son recovers, he'll meet someone going through pretty much the same thing he's suffering right now. He'll be able empathize with this person's suffering in ways you or I couldn't and give that person more credible hope than you or I ever could, simply because he'll have been through all this. In a word, he'll be a blessing to someone. And in being a blessing, he'll receive his blessing in return. Being a blessing out of the experience of our own suffering is what gives meaning to that suffering. Take a look at a crucifix some time and ask God to show you how that's true."

"Oh," his dad said thoughtfully, "no one ever explained it to me that way. I thought all these prayers and blessings you guys say were just so many fancy words that didn't really do anything."

"They may sound that way from time to time," I admitted, "but the words tell us of God's loving care for us and they're meant to be taken to heart. When they're prayed with fervor and really sink in, the words of God's blessing fuse with the experience of your own suffering in the crucible of your heart. The words and gestures of the unique blessing that only you can give is created in

---

14 https://w2.vatican.va/content/john-paul-ii/en/encyclicals/documents/hf_jp-ii_enc_30111980_dives-in-misericordia.html, December 30, 2016

that moment. When you share it with someone, God's love is expressed, and suffering is confronted by compassion. That's what blessings do."

"Blessings are how God and humans work together in the give and take of creation. I'll bet you can even find some words of blessing in your own heart right now to share with your wife and your son. You might not even need words; your presence could be enough to get the blessing across. You may even find that the suffering that's relieved by your blessing is not only his, but your own."

They looked at me and nodded. I blessed them and turned to leave. Looking back one last time as I got to the door, I saw that mom and dad had moved to their son's bedside, and were holding each other's hands, speaking together softly. They all looked up at me and smiled. It was pure goodness. The sense of God's presence was so thick you could reach out and touch it. If I'd taken a picture of the three of them just then, I'd be able to show you exactly what blessings look like in the flesh.

May the Lord bless you and keep you, and give us all the grace to be, like Mary, the blessings to each other God created us to be. Amen.

Questions For Discussion

1. Can you describe a time when what seemed at the time to be an affliction turned out to be a blessing in disguise?
2. What is it like for you to suffer?
3. How do you think we can best minister to people who are suffering?

Miracle

A while ago, a friend of mine told me about a time years before when he'd found out that his unmarried youngest daughter, away at college, was unexpectedly found to be with child.

"It was a tough time," he said. ""I saw myself as a failure as a dad. I wondered whether my wife and I had missed something bringing her up; I was angry with her, too. Those were bitter times. My daughter knew how I felt and couldn't face me. She felt she'd disgraced the family. Fortunately, my wife kept it all together; she worked hard trying to get me to calm down."

"I wasn't really hearing a bar of that song until the afternoon she called me and told me our daughter had been considering taking the baby's life and, my wife feared, maybe even her own. I remember that moment like it happened yesterday. Fortunately, my wife had convinced our daughter to call the right people, rushed up to the campus, and stayed with her until she knew she was safe. She asked me to join them the next day."

"I went out for a walk along the river later that day and stopped by the dam. I remember looking at the rushing water, leaves, and bubbles passing by, glistening in the fading sunlight and then going over the dam to disappear forever. Something changed inside me in that moment. I heard a whisper in my heart and suddenly I saw that absolutely everything in creation, especially life itself, was so miraculous and infinitely precious."

"'Why had it been so easy for me not to notice that?' I wondered. "How had I not seen that my baby girl and her baby were miracles too, far more beautiful and precious than any leaf or bubble? It occurred to me that my whole response up till then had been all about me. How I looked; what people would say about me; how hard it might be for me to face friends and family. I'd been angry and afraid about the trouble that would likely come along for me."

"Early the next day I drove up to my daughter's place on campus. I knocked on the door and she opened it. Her immediate response was terror, but only for an instant. She saw the tears in my eyes, and we rushed into each other's arms. I don't think I've ever embraced anyone like that. I was holding my lovely daughter with her innocent little baby growing inside, safe, alive and sobbing in my arms. The thought struck me like a thunderbolt: what had either of them ever done to me?"

"I asked her to forgive me and swore to her that we'd cherish her and her baby no matter what. Our Christmas that year was unforgettable. We all knew something about miracles and incarnation that we couldn't ever have imagined before, and we understood with precision how it is that love is both a commandment and a gift."

Questions For Discussion

1. Spend some time reflecting on the consistent ethic of life. What are the challenges to it that we face in difficult life situations?

2. Discuss abortion and assisted suicide. Look over the shoulder of each and consider what might motivate people to do such things?

3. What might our compassionate response be to people facing such choices?

Aneurysm

Does God really still manifest his power through ordinary folks like you and me? Let me tell you a story and you can decide for yourself.

A few years ago, I was working the overnight double shift as a volunteer hospital chaplain. It had been a pretty active night and around 3 a.m. I was beat. Then a call came from the neurotrauma ward. The family of a woman who had suffered a burst aneurysm in her head wanted spiritual support.

Wearily, I told God he was on his own for this one. I remember sensing that God was okay with that and actually had something interesting in mind, but I was too tired to think much about it. When I arrived in the family lounge, I found a large, anxious family that was all over the lot emotionally. Some were crying, others were laughing nervously, others were pretty quiet. We prayed together, the way we normally do.

As we finished our prayers, it occurred to me to ask everyone if they'd like to write mom a love letter or a prayer explaining how they felt just then. This way, I told them, when she got better, mom could see what everyone had been thinking and praying while she was out of it. In the moment, I realized this wasn't my idea at all. It was God's. If you haven't noticed in your own life by now, God has a way of making things "occur" to us.

The family liked that idea, so we spent about forty minutes writing. I wondered what I'd be doing with all those prayers and love letters when we got done. It didn't take long to find out.

From somewhere down deep, I found myself urged to ask again if they'd like to go read the prayers and love letters directly to mom. "She's unconscious," they said. "She won't hear us." Others said they thought that it might make them feel better, so I checked with the nursing staff first, and then off we went.

Mom was tied up to something to relieve the pressure in her brain. "We want to make that number come down," a nurse told me, pointing to a gauge, "or this won't have a happy ending." I asked everyone to grab or touch mom gently someplace and we'd read the prayers and love letters. They asked me to do the reading, since it was a pretty emotional moment for them.

So, that's what I did. I could tell folks liked doing that all together, but then I noticed something else. Mom was liking it too. The number on the brain pressure meter was going down. One by one we all became aware of that. I have no idea what was going on, but everyone knew Someone Else, Someone very big and very powerful and very gentle was there in the room together with us, and we all got real quiet, except for one man, who simply said "Wow."

I'm not going to suggest that a miracle occurred, but healing did, certainly among the family. There was liberation from the oppression of despair and helplessness. There was hope among the brokenhearted where there had been none just minutes before. The power of God's love, working through people and prayer, was up to something. We didn't know what it was, nor did we have to know anything other than that God's power was being shown to us, right in front of our eyes.

Questions For Discussion

1. When have you been too weary to offer consolation to someone? Did you turn the task over to God at the time? If you did, what was it like for you?

2. Have you ever experienced a miracle or something that seemed like a miracle to you?

3. Discuss miracles. Anything goes!

Chosen

As Saint Peter found out, the first moments after being chosen to do something utterly life-changing are both riveting and humbling. For many of us, being asked to be a wife or husband by someone is right up there in the list of things that completely grip us and fill us with awe. Wow — I remember thinking when it happened to me — someone actually wants to marry *me* — can you imagine?

For many of us, there are times we've been chosen for other things altogether, and the mission was quite different. I remember shortly after being chosen by the Selective Service, showing up at Fort Jackson, South Carolina, and being told face-to-face by a drill sergeant at the distance of about an eighth of an inch that the United States of America expected him to perform a miracle.

He asked if I would like to know what that miracle might be. Something told me he wasn't really asking that just to be polite, so I encouraged him to continue even though he was already explaining, in ways that only drill sergeants can, that the United States of America expected him to transform me from a worthless, undisciplined slug into a soldier.

Expressing doubts in his own words, which cannot be repeated here, about the probability of a successful outcome, he also told me I was also ugly and to get out of his sight. I happily complied, wondering uneasily what the next eight weeks were going to bring.

I also felt pretty small, thinking he was probably right about not being able to measure up. The Selective Service had chosen me, but surely, they'd been hallucinating if they thought that I'd come even close to being as good a soldier as that drill sergeant. What qualifications did I possess that were comparable to his, anyway?

So, I imagine what Peter must have felt after Jesus performed his miracle with the fish, and then chose Peter and his companions to follow him. I imagine they felt not too differently than me: called to do something we never thought we'd be doing, feeling absolutely unworthy and incapable of doing it, and wondering what the future would bring.

Unlike my drill sergeant though, Jesus didn't belittle Peter or tell him he was a slug and would never measure up. Nor did he correct Peter and say, "oh no, you're not a sinner, Peter," or anything like that. Arguably, Jesus knew perfectly well at some level what the trajectory of Peter's life would be. That doesn't come up either: Jesus simply tells Peter what his mission in life was going to be.

So it is with you and me. We've been chosen by God to be the ones through whom God's love is to be expressed in the world at this time. That's the mission. That's why you and I are here. It really isn't any more complicated than that.

If we feel unqualified or unworthy, then a) we're right and b) it doesn't matter. The principal thing is to accept that mission and become more God-conscious than self-conscious as we move through life. It's to become aware of and to consent to the presence and action of God within us, understanding as the prophet Isaiah pointed out millennia ago, that it is God who accomplishes all that we do, anyway.

The challenge for you and me is to let go and allow God to act through and within us as God needs to in the moment. The story of humanity is far larger than the story of any individual human, and little if any of it ever turns out exactly as we imagine it should. Indeed, in this moment, is life unfolding just the way you thought it would?

We've all likely heard the expression by now– if you want to make God laugh, tell him your plans. It may just be that you and I, like Peter and his companions, have been chosen by God for a destiny we can't even begin to imagine and truly don't see, even though it's actually in play.

Thomas Merton expressed it this way in a famous prayer many of you have probably memorized by now:

"My Lord God I have no idea where I am going. I do not see the road ahead of me. I cannot know for certain where it will end. Nor do I really know myself, and the fact that I think I am following your will does not mean that I am actually doing so.

But I believe that my desire to please you does in fact please you. And I hope that I have that desire in all that I am doing. I hope that I will never do anything apart from that desire. And I know that if I do this you will lead me by the right road though I may know nothing about it.

Therefore, will I trust you always though I may seem to be lost and in the shadow of death. I will not fear, for you are ever with me, and you will never leave me to face my perils alone."[15]

You and I, like Peter, have been given a fabulous destiny far beyond our ability to grasp. If we were to see it now, right in front of us, we would likely recoil in terror, awe and astonishment, consumed with fears of unworthiness and incapability.

Yet that's exactly what God would like to give us as a gift. All that's required is, in utter humility and acceptance, to respond "yes, Lord, I have no idea what it is for which I'm signing up, but I know you're all about love, so I will trust you the way I did before I even existed.[16] You've chosen me. Here I am. Do with me as you will."

Questions For Discussion

1. How does your life express God's love?
2. How do you see God's love expressed in other people?
3. Are you comfortable "letting go and letting God?" What inhibitions and reservations do you detect in yourself and others?

---

15 https://www.goodreads.com/quotes/80913-my-lord-god-i-have-no-idea-where-i-am, March 1, 2019
16 Meister Eckhart

Satisfaction Of The Deepest Longing

While we might wonder from time to time how we ended up with the friends we have, there's a lot of truth in the remark that at the root of all friendship lies a longing of some kind.

Do you remember the first step you took? The very first step can be hard for some folks, especially the shy, because it involves the risk of misunderstanding and rejection. You know in that moment that you're quite vulnerable, but perhaps that indescribable longing convinced you that it was worth the effort. I suspect that most of us know, having been on the sending or receiving end, that there's no more poignant sadness than an offer of friendship misunderstood or rejected.

It's exactly into that realm of risk that God perennially enters with humanity. To establish friendship with us, God is willing to risk misunderstanding and rejection, all the way up to its most violent and degrading manifestation as crucifixion.

Let me tell you a little story. My friend Paul is a very shy guy. As a kid, he told me, he used to hide under his bed when his parents brought home friends from the office or other folks not in the family. There were plenty of reasons for Paul to have felt poorly about himself, but that's another story altogether, and not a pretty one.

Making friends came hard for Paul as he grew up, and he was frequently misunderstood because he just didn't have it in him to be out there like other folks. An unfortunate reality of the human condition is that the default response of most folks to very quiet people is that those quiet folks have no use for anyone, which in many cases is exactly the opposite of their deepest desire, which is simply to be loved, and gently accepted as-is.

I asked Paul one day how he ever ended up married with six kids.

"It wasn't my idea," he explained. "Mary Lou did all the heavy lifting."

"How so?" I asked.

"She had read something I wrote for one of our high school magazines," Paul explained. "She told me much later that she had seen something she liked about me very much in the poems I wrote. We laughed and I recalled how I was at the time, and how I could never have dreamt of expressing anything like that aloud to anyone."

"Then what happened?" I asked.

"She told me she realized she was going to have to take matters into her own hands," Paul said, "So I started getting notes from her. At first, I didn't know what to make of it, but somehow, I began to look forward to getting them. They met some deep longing in me — something I couldn't name but wanted very much."

"I started writing notes back. Pretty crummy ones, but Mary Lou was so kind and patient. One day, I actually got up the courage to mumble 'Hi' to her as we passed in the hall at school. I didn't think I really had it in me. I remember blushing and feeling like an idiot even as the words left my mouth. Why would she ever want to hear from someone like me, anyway? I was so afraid of being rejected."

"How did she take it?" I asked.

"She smiled and said 'Hi, Paul,' back to me. She used my name, Tim. It sounded as if she had known me forever. I felt as if I was in the presence of something amazing and miraculous. She had accepted my stupid 'hello' and I wanted just to stand there forever, gaze on that lovely smile of hers and listen to her say 'hello' back to me endlessly. Sounds crazy, doesn't it?"

"Not at all, Paul," I reassured him.

"You know, Tim," Paul said, "that was a redemptive moment for me. My whole life was different after that. It took a while, but we became such good friends. We wanted to know everything about each other, and she was so compassionate with me when I talked about all my troubles and insecurities growing up."

"When we were apart, I felt this emptiness, this thirst. Even now, after forty years and six children, she's like my second self — no, even better than that; closer. Maybe it's like that with us and God, too, what do you think?"

I told him I agreed.

Like Mary Lou with Paul, Jesus realized we'd never get to know God as God really is unless God took the initiative.

Like Paul, Peter, James, and John wanted to stay forever on the mountain where they'd witnessed the Transfiguration, but life doesn't work like that. As with the best of friendships, there was much more to be done, deeper depths to be explored, longings to be satisfied, and identities to be fully realized.

From the Transfiguration onward in the New Testament, it becomes increasingly clear that at some profound depth your deepest identity and mine is located in Christ and indistinguishable from him. As Saint Catherine of Genoa said, "My deepest me is God." It's an identity of astonishing beauty. We're not God, but we're made out of God. Listen to Thomas Merton describe this identity:

"At the center of our being is a point of nothingness which is untouched by sin and illusion, a point of pure truth, a point or spark that belongs entirely to God, which is never at our disposal, from which God disposes of our lives, which is inaccessible to the fantasies of our own mind or the brutalities of our own will."

"This little point of nothingness and of absolute poverty is the pure glory of God written within us.... It is like a pure diamond blazing with the invisible light of heaven. It is in everybody, and if we could see it, we would see these billions of points of light coming together in the blaze of a sun that would make all the darkness and cruelty of life vanish completely.

"I have no program for this kind of seeing. It is only given. But the gate of heaven is everywhere."[17]

That's our deepest identity, reflecting the glory of the transfigured Lord. It's pretty amazing, so amazing I'd bet very few of us ever thought we really had it in us.

---

17 Thomas Merton, *A Merton Reader*, ed. Thomas P. McDonnell (New York: Image Books, 1989), p.347

Questions For Discussion

1. Are you now, or have you ever been shy? What was that experience like for you and how do you, or did you, address it?
2. Merton remarked that "the gate of heaven is everywhere." Would you agree? Why or why not?
3. What are the differences between our identity and our roles and occupations in life? What problems might arise if we view ourselves as "human doings" rather than "human beings?"
4. What's it like for you when you reflect on your own deepest identity?

Taz

After Jesus was raised, things were irrevocably different, and so they remain today. Instead of being local just to a specific body, Jesus Christ, through his Holy Spirit, is everywhere. Superficially it may not seem that way, but for those who come to see that the inevitable consequence of obedience to the law of love is resurrection, things can never be the same again.

But some things do appear to remain the same to those who don't grasp what's different after resurrection. So it is that we have the gospel of poor Thomas, who will be remembered for all time as the person who didn't accept the bodily resurrection of Jesus.

I hope that none of us feels sorry for Thomas, let alone superior to him, because his story clearly expresses the willingness of Jesus to straighten out people like that: people who honestly express their doubts about resurrection, yet are willing to stick around long enough to have those doubts resolved.

The Jesuit theologian Gerald O'Collins has written quite a bit about what it might be like to be resurrected, suggesting that our resurrected bodies would likely be "a gathering up and coming together of our whole accumulated past. In resurrection, by the power of God our time and history will be summed up and completed." [18] Resurrection's very much about communication and relationship in ways that were simply not possible before. We need an identifiable presence to be able to engage in that, and bodily resurrection supplies what's needed.

Setting aside for the moment what we *think* we ought to say we believe, let's consider exactly what we *do* feel and think in total honesty, like Doubting Thomas, at the precise moment we hear the phrase "Jesus Christ is risen from the dead." Please do that thinking right now.

Well, what was it like? Some of us may find that in all honesty, not much separates us from Doubting Thomas. If that's the case, hold those feelings honestly and present them to the Lord for resolution with confident trust in God's love, for there's truly no point in saying we believe in something when we really have

---

18 Gerald O'Collins,"Our Risen Selves", *America Magazine*, April 9, 2012, p.11ff

doubts. But do stick around — there's no doubt that your story will end at least as well as Thomas' did, though it may come to you as something of a shock, as it did to him.

One of our neighbors cheerfully gave me permission to tell you this story about them, which vividly suggests what that resurrection shock might be like. They also said I could use their names if I wanted to, and I do, so here we go.

The Treacys have a skinny, black cat named Taz. He has a few odd white markings on his head and fancy white paws. We all like Taz because Taz keeps the neighborhood mouse-free. His owners don't like him as much because he likes to bring all our dead mice home to them.

If he happens to come home empty-handed, Taz scratches at the door until someone lets him in. Glowering at everyone, he takes a sip or two of water from his dish, then goes upstairs to someone's bed and takes it over.

One day, some of the neighborhood kids were coming home on the school bus, and one of them happened to be looking out the window as the bus slowed down to turn off Route 44 onto Breezy Hill Road. He caught a glimpse of a black cat lying on the side of the road, dead.

Now the only black cat in the neighborhood was Taz, as far as he knew, so he ran to our neighbor crying, "Mrs. Treacy, Mrs. Treacy, Taz is dead, Taz is dead!" Helen ran down to Route 44 close enough to the body to see what she needed to see, then ran home again and tearfully called her husband to come home, get the cat and bury it. In the meantime, she gathered her crying children around her and consoled them as best she could, for they were very upset.

Now, Greg's a compassionate guy, so home he came, picked up the cat from the highway with a snow shovel and took it to their backyard, where it was laid to rest next to the family's previous cat. After a few cat prayers, they assembled tearfully inside and consoled each other with stories of what a fabulous cat Taz had been. It was a very sad scene indeed.

Then there was a scratch at the door. The room went dead quiet, and everyone looked at each other with alarm. Was that really a scratch they'd just heard or were their minds playing tricks with them? Then the scratching came again. So, the way it works in most households, everyone turned expectantly to mom.

Helen told me she gasped and thought "Don't do this to me, God!" Then she approached the door with fear and trepidation. Opening the door just a crack, she looked down and there he was: Taz, with those odd white markings on his head and those fancy white paws.

As Helen screamed, Taz looked up at her as if to say "What's the problem, lady? Get out of the way and let me in." Stunned, her body automatically opened the door a bit more and the cat walked in, threw a "What's wrong with you guys?" look at the family that was staring at him with wide-open mouths and eyes like silver dollars, went over to its dish, got a sip of water and then headed up the stairs to someone's room to take over a bed.

It was a few moments before anyone could speak, but then the room burst into a cacophony of tears, laughter, exclamations like "What did you bury back there, Greg, a skunk?!" and all sorts of other things. There was great joy in the Treacy household just then, maybe not all that different from what the disciples felt when they encountered the resurrected Jesus.

Now Taz didn't die and experience resurrection the way Jesus did, but Helen says that for an instant that's *exactly* what seemed to be happening. She says she'll never forget the shock she felt the moment they first heard scratching at the door.

I asked her to tell me more about that moment and she said it was an explosive mixture of incredulity — this can't be happening; hope — I sure hope it's happening, and cognitive dissonance — this absolutely impossible thing is happening right here, right now, right in front of me!

In that breakthrough moment, the family shared all the feelings of every Christian who has ever wondered about the resurrection and suddenly experienced that beautiful instant when it becomes blindingly clear that yes, not only **can** Jesus be with us at the deepest level of what it means to be me and you, but it's way better than you and I had ever hoped, and it's happening right now. Suddenly, it's the doubtful viewpoints that're incredible; those views that somehow, we're separated from God, that Jesus died a long time ago and won't be around again for who knows how long.

Maybe you can see the deep truth of resurrection in your own life, right now. I see the resurrected Jesus at the hospital all the time. You can't miss him at school, and you aren't paying attention if you miss him at work. Jesus asked Thomas to reach inside his wounds, for that's where the convincing truth's to be found.

Look *inside* your joy; look inside your suffering; look *inside* your virtue and look *inside* your sin. Reach all the way into life, the way Thomas put his hands into Jesus' wounds, and believe; enter into the suffering, and enter into the joy.

The resurrected Jesus is all over the place, present and acting in you and me, through you and me, and for you and me, doing all the same things everywhere the way he did back when he could only do it in his own body. When it finally hits home, it will feel like a shock to your whole being, just as it did for Helen, because the resurrected Jesus truly died but is in this moment very much alive.

Don't grasp it 100% yet? That's perfectly okay, Thomas the apostle didn't either. Just remember to stick around and open up when you hear God scratching at your door.

Questions For Discussion

1. What does "resurrection" mean to you?
2. Has something "impossible" ever happened to you? What was that experience like?
3. Have you ever had imitations of resurrection joy? If you have, what was that like for you? If you haven't, what do you think they might be like?

Palm Sunday

There's a story about a young dad named Ted and his two children that I'd like to share with you because it happened one Palm Sunday as they were leaving church a few years ago. Ted's son Tommy turned to him and asked: "How come Jesus had to die?" His sister Susie joined in, "Yeah dad, how come Jesus had to suffer and die like that? Wasn't he God?"

Ted thought about it for a moment and then told his two teenagers: "Well, it's like this: in Jesus, as a pure, undeserved gift, God became what humans are so that humans could become what God is. All humans die, so it stands to reason that Jesus had to die too. But Jesus died in a special way that made up for our sins so that we could be happy with God forever." He could tell from their expressions that Tommy and Susie weren't particularly happy with that answer.

Recalling his Catholic school training from many years ago he went on: "Let me try explaining it differently. A long time ago, Saint Anselm wrote that when humans turned away from God in what we call the original sin of Adam and Eve, that was *so* big a mistake that only God could correct it. The only possible compensation *to* God for something like that was for someone as *big* as God to undo for us what had been done. Now, since humans had to undo what humans did, and Jesus was both fully God and fully human, he had to suffer and die on behalf of us all, since that was the punishment a mistake like that deserved."

Susie and Tommy looked at their dad with faces that told him his wheels were getting stuck in the sand. Fortunately his wife, Alice, was there too, so she told the kids "Look, God loved the world so much that even when we were all in the middle of the biggest mistake we could possibly make, God came to us as a human in Jesus Christ to us to save us from it. And as dad said, part of being human is that all humans die."

"But why did Jesus have to die on the *cross*, mom?" Susie asked. "He could've done it some less painful way. You're not telling me why he had to die like that."

"Let's take a little trip," Ted suggested after a few moments. "I have an idea that might help explain everything." They all got into their car and Ted drove to a nearby cemetery. They all got out and walked up to a veterans' memorial that was there.

"See this?" Ted asked his children. "It's a memorial to the veterans who died defending our country. Look at the inscription: 'Greater love hath no man than to lay down his life for his friends.' Do you know who first said that?"

The children shook their heads "no."

"Jesus," Ted told them, "just before he suffered and died for us. Just as the soldiers and sailors died for love of our country, Jesus died for love of all humankind. If the soldiers and sailors had not been willing to die, our enemies would have destroyed us."

Tommy and Susie took that in silently. Then Susie asked, "So if Jesus hadn't been willing to die, our enemies would've destroyed us, too. What kind of enemies do we have, anyway, and where are they?"

Ted pondered what to say next, but Alice took the ball before he could speak.

"Who did the veterans fight?" she asked.

"Other countries," the children said together, naming a few.

Seeing where Alice was going, Ted asked: "Who's the enemy Jesus fights?"

"The devil?" Tommy suggested.

"Bad people?" Susie asked.

"You're both right, in a way," Ted said, "but there's a sure-fire tool you can always use to find the enemy that Jesus fights. It's a funny kind of tool though, because you can also use it to see who Jesus' friends are."

"Show us!" the children shouted.

Ted took them over to the car and had them peer into the side view mirror.

"Wait a minute, Dad — we're not the enemy," the children exclaimed with horror, looking in the mirror, "we love Jesus!"

"Of course, you do, and so do mom and I," Ted said, "Remember, I told you the tool can be used to find Jesus' friends just as easily as his enemies. Here's how it works: a mirror always reflects back exactly what's in front of it without distortion. An enemy of Jesus is any person who looks into the mirror and sees a person staring back who says in his heart 'I don't need God,' 'I make my own reality,' 'I make my own rules.' In a nutshell, it's the sin of Adam and Eve. A friend is any person who looks in the mirror and sees…"

"The self he really wants to be?" Tommy interrupted.

"Wow, Tommy," Ted said, "that was pretty deep — where'd you get that from?"

Tommy just shook his head and said, "I don't know."

"Well, you're right, Ted continued. "Let me go even further. A friend of Jesus looks into the mirror and sees someone who looks ,for all the world, just like Jesus himself. He sees someone loving, compassionate, patient, and kind looking back out of that mirror; a person who knows that he or she needs God more than food or water; a person happy to serve others just as Jesus did."

"The enemy Jesus fights is indeed the devil and his ancient lie that we have no need of God. Maybe a big reason Jesus had to die is hidden in that letter Saint Paul wrote, especially the part where it says Jesus 'emptied himself.' When he emptied himself, he made room for us. He created space within himself for us so we could see from his perspective what dying to pride and self-importance looks like."

"One of the most painful things we can do in life is to witness the humiliation and death of our false understanding of ourselves — to admit without trying to hide anything or soften it up, just how proud and wrong we were. Thankfully we have Jesus to cling to for comfort while we're going through it. It's a good thing God's not into blame and retaliation!"

"The amazing thing," Alice explained, "is that when Jesus defeats his enemies, they don't die — they surrender of their own free will and live. So, when we say Jesus saves us from our sins, it means Jesus saved us from our self-imposed separation from God. Surrendering is like walking across the bridge Jesus built out of himself, over the river of death, that connects what's human like us to what's divine, like God."

"This is a lot to think about, Dad," Tommy said, nodding to his sister. "It's going to be a long time before we really get it, I think."

"You're probably right, Tommy," his dad agreed. "It'll take a lifetime, but that's what lifetimes are actually all about."

Questions For Discussion

1. Why do you think Jesus had to die?
2. What are the fruits of blame and retaliation? How well do they work as solutions?
3. What is it about us that dies? How does you answer make you feel?

Making A Name For Yourself

Everyone wants to make a name for himself, or herself, as the case may be. It's the phrase we use to describe the process of being and becoming who we are. Everyone wants to be remembered for some accomplishment, some contribution, some distinctive mark that we've left on the world. For what would you wish to be remembered?

The folks who built the tower of Babel thought they'd like to be remembered as the people who could reach to the heavens, where the gods lived. The story itself is quite old, and probably was lifted in whole or part from pagan mythologies contemporary with early Israel. The source doesn't really matter all that much, because the story's turned to a new purpose in the Hebrew scriptures.

The key phrase in the tale is "…let us make a name for ourselves." While that might have been a worthwhile goal in pagan religions, it flies in the face of the special relationship that Israel has with God. For Israelites, the phrase would properly have been "…let **God** make a name for us," not "…let **us** make a name for ourselves." Isaiah says, for example, "…it is he [God] who has accomplished all we have done."

Note carefully that the passage from Isaiah doesn't suggest that we sit back and let God do everything on his own out there someplace — it's a lot more personal. God accomplishes everything we do through us, as *we* act in daily life. The key is to trust God and allow God to operate within us, letting God make a name for us rather than deciding it's us who have to make a name for ourselves. It's actually more a case of simply becoming aware of God acting within us than of us granting permission, but either perspective will do.

Granting this permission, or arriving at this awareness, is fundamental to our understanding the purpose of the Eucharist, where we receive God objectively into our bodies, and crucial to our understanding of the Holy Spirit, where we let the God we have received now act in and through us by means of his Holy Spirit.

I've got a story for you that shows how that works these days, but I need to explore just one more thing with you before I tell it. You know, a reasonable person might ask how we can tell that God's Holy Spirit is actively at work within us. Saint Paul helps us out quite a bit there in Galatians, telling us that the fruits of the Spirit are peace and joy, love and patience, kindness and generosity, faithfulness, gentleness, and self-control. If we see any combination of these virtues in our life, then we have objective proof that the Holy Spirit is indeed working in us.

Let me connect the threads and tell you that story now. You might remember those terrible snowstorms we had a few years ago that knocked out everyone's electricity for so long. As it turned out, I was the on-call chaplain at the hospital that night. As you might imagine, I got no sleep. The emergency department was full of man vs. chain saw, carbon monoxide poisoning, and lots more.

Anyway, in the middle of all that, a person passed away in one of the ICUs upstairs. I got called, and the nurse said there were two family members who would appreciate some prayers. I told them I'd be up as soon as possible but warned that it would be a while.

A little more than an hour later I was able to break away gently from the other folks and headed on up to the ICU. On the way up, I told God that I was completely out of energy and that he'd have to handle this one all by himself. God was fine with that.

The relatives, a woman who also happened to be a nurse, and her husband, were not happy that it had been over an hour since they'd called. There are ways to deal with that, of course, and in a few moments we all moved on to the room where her fifty-year-old baby brother lay dead. I expressed my condolences, and we prayed a bit together. Then I asked what he had been like.

We began to chat in greater depth, and as the conversation unfolded, it emerged that her older sister had died just a few months earlier. She, with her husband, was now all alone. Her brother had suffered tremendously most of his life, from cancer, diabetes, blindness, lost limbs — just about everything you could imagine. He'd remained faithful and as cheerful as he could be through it all. His sister had loved him very much, and she was angry; her brother's lifetime of suffering seemed just so unfair.

Her husband quietly reflected that anger. We prayed a bit more and stood silently together. Then it happened.

I had no intention of saying anything, but God did. What came out of my mouth next was nothing I had planned, nothing I would ever have dreamed of saying and certainly nothing anyone had trained me to say. I turned to the woman and asked, "Would you like to see where your brother is right now?"

The moment those words came out of my mouth my gut wrenched and my mind exploded with astonished disbelief at what I had just said. "What did you say *that* for, genius!!" roared my brain. "What are you going to do now, part the heavens?" Almost instantly though, I felt God gently, yet powerfully communicate to me — "Be still. Just watch."

The woman must have thought I'd lost it because looked at me as if I had five heads and glanced worriedly at her husband, who was doing the same back to her. I guess they saw that I was between them and the door and that for their own safety they should probably just say "Yes," and so they did.

At this point I became a spectator, wondering how it was all going to end up myself.

I watched myself tell them "His entire life was like this," as my arms rose from my side as if I were on a crucifix, "filled with suffering, like Jesus." I couldn't have prevented my arms from going up; it was as if they were attached to someone else. All I could do was watch. Then I, or more accurately, someone else motioned to them to draw near and I hugged both of their heads close to my chest and said, "Now his head is resting happily upon the heart of Jesus, just… like… this."

We stayed there like that for just a few moments and then I gently released them. The woman's husband was crying. She herself had a look unlike anything I had ever seen before in my life. It was as if in that moment, everything had become clear; somehow, everything made sense; somehow, everything was okay. Yes, of course that's where her brother was right now.

We didn't say much more, and I excused myself to go back the inferno unfolding in the emergency department, telling them to ask the nurse to call me if they needed me again for anything.

Later that evening, I saw them once more as they walked through the lobby back out to their car. We saw each other and they smiled, waving at me. I recall that there might have even been a laugh, but a deep, knowing laugh, not one of those nervous kinds of things. God had indeed accomplished all I had done for them that evening. You could've reached out and touched the presence of the Holy Spirit.

I prayed in that moment a deeply awed, humble prayer of thanksgiving. Maybe you've done the same when you've been a conduit of the Holy Spirit in your life, too. I realized then that's how God, working in and through us is the one who actually accomplishes all that we have done, making a name both for himself and for us; and that the name he makes for himself and for us is love.

Questions For Discussion

1. What kind of name do you wish to make for yourself? Why?
2. Have you ever experienced a moment when God has commandeered your being for God's purposes?
3. What kind of name would people have for you? Does it matter to you what it might be? Why?

Cannibals, Magic, and Real Presence

My friend Ernie has a daughter, Alice, who has never had an unexpressed thought. Among the many other benefits of this phenomenon is that Alice keeps Ernie on his toes about his faith. One day on the way home after mass, Alice had a question for Ernie.

"Sandy on my softball team says that Catholics are all cannibals, Dad. Are we?"

"What are you talking about?" Ernie asked.

"Cannibals eat other people, Sandy says, and we Catholics say we eat the body and blood of Jesus, so that makes us cannibals," Alice replied. "Is she right?"

"Not really," Ernie said, "For starters, cannibals eat folks whether they want to be eaten or not. Jesus offered himself to us voluntarily, and actually insisted that we take a bite."

"But all cannibals eat humans, and Jesus was a human, so that makes us cannibals, doesn't it?" Alice pressed.

"Don't forget that Jesus is human and divine, Alice," Ernie said. "His one person connects the two natures in himself. By offering his whole being for all people and all time, he offers us the connection he himself is between the human and the divine, and all kinds of things become possible. If we don't accept the human part, we miss out on the connection to the divine. No cannibal gets to enjoy that — it is food that can only be given by love, not taken by force."

"But you're still talking food, Dad, so that makes us cannibals," Alice insisted.

"Is all food the same, Alice?" Ernie asked.

Alice sensed a trap coming up, so she said "Yes and no."

"When you eat some Chicken McNuggets™, what happens next, Alice?" Ernie asked.

"I get indigestion," Alice replied.

"In addition to getting sick, your bodies nourished a little, right?" Ernie continued.

"Probably a little bit," Alice agreed reluctantly.

"Do you then start to grow feathers and lay eggs?" Ernie prodded.

"You're weird, Dad," Alice replied.

"That's a difference then, isn't it?" Ernie asked. "We don't become chickens or even anything like chickens after we eat those McNuggets, but after we receive the body and blood of Christ, we're connected to God through Christ and energized to become inclined, if not even eager, to love and serve folks around us," Ernie said. "We do become more like Jesus, and able to do what he did because we're connected to God and our community in a very special way."

"I don't feel special every time I receive," Alice admitted.

"Me neither," Ernie sympathized, "but just the way our bodies take in food and use it for the different needs of the trillions of cells that make up our bodies and we're not aware of any of that, so the connection with God plays out with our spirit when we receive Communion. We don't have to be aware of what's going on at all, but man, when we *do* become aware, even a little bit, everything changes."

"Everything?" Alice asked, eyebrows raised.

"Yep," Ernie replied, "Everything. When the focus goes off me and onto God, the reason I do anything changes to the reason God would do anything. When I intentionally appropriate the sacrament the way God invites us to, it all becomes totally about love."

"I'll have to tell Sandy that," Alice said.

"Aside from telling us we're cannibals, did Sandy have any other wisdom to share with you, Alice?" Ernie asked.

"Oh yes," Alice answered, "she also told me we Catholics practice magic."

"Magic?" Ernie asked.

"Sandy said we believe that when a priest says some magic words over the bread and wine, they become Jesus. That's magic," Alice said.

"Hmm," Ernie mused. "I wonder what she thinks about the words in something like a naturalization ceremony. Remember when Mr. Massoud across the way became a citizen?"

"I remember that — it was a great party," Alice recalled.

"It was more than just a great party, Alice," Ernie said. "He had to take an oath of allegiance to the United States before a judge to do that. Up until the moment he spoke, he was a citizen of Lebanon. The moment he finished, he was instantly an American. Everything, as he will tell you himself, changed completely in an instant. Was that magic, Alice? I wonder what Sandy would say?"

"I'll have to ask her that, too," Alice said.

"Why don't you invite her to come with us to mass next week, Alice?" Ernie suggested. "She won't have to bring a knife and a fork. And there's nothing like seeing a real magic act by a real magician!"

"Father Joe isn't a magician," Alice said.

"No, he's not," Ernie said. "The bread and wine become the body and blood, soul and divinity of Jesus because Jesus said that's what would happen when Father Joe pronounces the words of consecration over them."

"It's similar in a certain way to Mr. Massoud's becoming a US citizen because the laws of the people of the United States say that's what happens when you take the oath of allegiance," Ernie explained.

"His future is completely different now than it would be if he were back in Lebanon. Likewise, our future is completely different now than it would be if we had never consumed the real presence of Jesus. There's no magic there anymore than there's magic in the oath of allegiance, but there is enormous significance in both cases. Funny how easy it is to take those enormous privileges of being Americans and being children of God for granted."

The real presence of Jesus in the Eucharist may indeed be a reality difficult for many to embrace. Perhaps the best approach to dealing with that discomfort is to choose to allow the reality of the real presence to embrace us and let that happen on God's terms and in God's time.

We may just find that instead of being cannibals or magicians, we are actually citizens of a fabulous nation of people who have been gifted with the unconditional love of one who is pleased to give us his entire self, asking nothing of you and me in return except to give him our own entire selves right back and delight in the explosion of miracles that follows.

Questions For Discussion

1. Do you think words have power? If so, can you describe a scenario or two in which you've see that power exercised?
2. What's your take on the real presence? Do you honestly believe it to be so?
3. Saint Peter Chrysologos remarked that we will not be allowed to keep what we do not give away. How might that comment apply to our reception of the Eucharist?

Digital Possession

The question posed by the young man in the gospel who asked Jesus what he had to do to inherit eternal life is pretty straightforward. The answer's simple, too — respond appropriately to the love of God. But life's complicated, isn't it, and it's easy to get distracted. Let's take a look today at distraction and its much more powerful first cousin, possession.

As most of you know, I spend a fair amount of time over at the hospital as a chaplain. One day, one of the other chaplains was telling me about a patient who happened to be in a lot of pain. "He doesn't seem to be able to put any distance between himself and the disease," my fellow chaplain told me, "I wonder whether he has the disease, or the disease has him."

I found out for myself later on that the patient's pain had powerfully possessed him. I was reminded, being with him, of the last days of Saint Thérèse of Lisieux, whose excruciating pain had possessed her so completely that she was too distracted even to be able to think of God. The phrase my fellow chaplain had used stuck with me long after the visit. Does he have the disease or does the disease have him? It seemed to me to be an observation that we could validly make with regard to other kinds of possessions that distract us too, especially those that might overtly or much more subtly distract us from God.

Jesus points out something like that with regard to material possessions, too. Do we have the possessions with which we've been blessed, or do they possess us? Is our happiness enmeshed with our possessions or do we derive our happiness from the loving intimacy we enjoy with God, our family and our friends?

It's a crucial question. One day, we *will* leave this world and be forcibly detached from our material possessions whether we like it or not, to be possessed by God or possessed perhaps by something else altogether. Are we well enough detached from our stuff that we could give it all up without feeling sad and withdrawing from God as the young man did, or have our possessions got a lock on us? Who indeed owns who? Think for a moment about your own possessions. Is there anything you'd feel sad about having to give up? While you're thinking, let me tell you another story.

My friend Ernie told me one day he was so taken by the gravity of this issue that he decided he was going to find out just who had who in his family. Conjuring up a plan, he explained it to his wife, Frances, who told him he was probably crazy, but agreed to go along with it anyway.

Early the next day, his daughter Alice came to the breakfast table and asked if anyone had seen her iPhone.

"I have it," Ernie said.

"Thanks, Dad," Alice said, "Just toss it into my bag, would you?"

"No," Ernie replied.

"What?" Alice asked, stopping in her tracks. "Don't be goofy, Dad. Just do it, please, I need to catch the bus."

"Your mother and I have decided the family needs a digital fast," Ernie explained, as their son Tommy came downstairs with the same question as his sister.

"How are we supposed to stay in touch with anyone?" Tommy asked, astonished.

"Talk to them in person," Ernie suggested.

"I've never heard of anything so stupid," Alice fumed, squinting at Ernie. "I bet you get to keep your phone, don't you?"

"No," Ernie said, "Your mother and I gave our phones to Deacon Tim, along with yours. He's going to hold on to them for a week; we're going on a digital fast."

That didn't go over well at all, and the dialogue that followed is not suitable for repetition in a sacred place, so let's just say Tommy and Alice were furious and exceedingly sad, not unlike our young friend in the gospel. They went off to school in a murderous mood.

Frances came in from walking the dog after they'd left, as planned.

"How'd it go?" she asked Ernie.

"Pretty much the way we expected," Ernie said. "Let's see what happens next."

"I really do want to check my Facebook, Ernie," Frances said. "I might be missing something important."

"What's good for the goose is good for the gander," Ernie said firmly, and Frances reluctantly agreed.

The kids came home from school that day to find the computers and iPads in the family room and empty shelves where the TVs used to be.

"You can use them for homework, but that's it," Ernie and Frances explained. "We'll be here to make sure that's all you do."

The week wore on, and on Saturday I came by with the phones.

"What was it like?" I asked the family as we shared a cup of coffee and some cookies.

Tommy spoke first. "I felt like I didn't have my shoes on, the first day," he said. "My friends wondered why I didn't know about things. They looked at me strangely, like I had a disease or something."

"Me, too," Alice said, "I felt like I was being punished for something I didn't do."

"My girlfriends at the gym thought it was strange at first," Frances said, "but then more than one admitted that they wished they weren't tethered to their phones like dogs on a leash. The phones had them — they didn't have the phones. One of them did get angry though and told me I was married to a Neanderthal," Meg said, turning to Ernie with an affectionate grin.

"My boss was not amused," Ernie admitted. "He told me to go find some other way to prove how holy I was to everyone."

"Anything else?" I asked, chewing a cookie. The family pondered that request for a moment.

"I think somehow I got to find out who my true friends were," Tommy said after a bit. "I think they were the ones who took time to spend time with me in person. The rest kind of blew me off. I wondered whether they had ever been real friends at all."

"Same with me," Alice said. "At first, I was anxious and upset, but then I got used to being around just a few of my best friends: you know, the compassionate ones. They told me everything I needed to know to get by. When we talked face-to-face, we really connected deeply. I was surprised how shallow some of my friendships had become. At first, I was sad because I didn't have my phone, but at the end of the week I was sad about something else — something I'd lost, actually given up voluntarily. My phone had me. I didn't have the phone, and it had taken me to a dark superficial place where nothing serious ever came up. I felt so *real* sometimes during the week, and even found myself thinking about God. It felt good. Just getting a little distance between me and the phone let me see what a big distraction it can become, if I let it."

The family nodded in agreement, each in turn telling me in their own words that pretty much anything that distracted them from awareness of living in the presence of God was probably not a good thing.

Ernie tells me everyone has their phones again now and uses them freely, but not the way they had before. "It's just a tool we can take or leave now," Ernie said. "We have our phones now — they don't have us. We're learning to see our other possessions that way, too."

Two thousand years on, the lure of possessions remains with us, even though their appearances may have changed. Not everyone needs to go on a digital diet, but the gospel challenges us, as it has challenged millions of people for thousands of years, to put some distance between ourselves and any possessions that possess us, from anything that distracts us from an intimate relationship with God; any enslavement that stands between us and what we must do to inherit eternal life.

Questions For Discussion

1. How would a "digital diet" go over in your situation?
2. In what ways can we know if our possessions possess us?
3. If you are "connected" through email, Facebook and such like, how do you treat people who are not?
4. If you're *not* connected, how does it feel to be surrounded by those who are?
5. How does the Eucharist connect everyone? How might you compare that connection to a digital one?

Pinocchio

This month, back in 1883, Carlo Collodi finished writing a wonderful little children's story that I'm sure everyone here has heard. See if you can guess what it is — it starts like this: "*Once upon a time, there was ...'A king!' my little readers will say right away. No, children, you are wrong. Once upon a time there was a piece of wood....*"

Of course, the story is *Pinocchio*, and it's about how the piece of wood was carved into a puppet who, after a series of adventures, became the real little boy his creator, the woodcarver, had always longed for.

Collodi had not started out to write a children's story. He was a journalist and *Pinocchio* was actually a social allegory dealing with some very serious themes. In fact, in the original version, Pinocchio dies a horrible death — hanged for his innumerable faults, at the end of Chapter 15.

Collodi eventually wrote a number of additional chapters, in which the Blue Fairy rescued Pinocchio and eventually transformed him into a real boy, but only after he had earned the privilege.

If we've heard the story, we remember Pinocchio listening to the cat and the fox, that tempted him with dreams of unearned pleasure, glory, and wealth. Their intent of course was simply for them to enrich themselves, and they laughed at Pinocchio with evil glee as he willingly gave in to their temptations, and they lied and stole at his expense.

As the story proceeded, things went from bad to worse, and Pinocchio met what seemed like an endless series of misfortunes, watched his nose grow as he tried his hand at lying, and eventually turned into a donkey on the Island of Pleasure as he learned what happened to those who give in to the temptations of idleness and self-gratification.

It wasn't until he was in the belly of the beast and met his father who had been looking for him all along, that he came to see what the cost of giving in to those temptations had been to the one he loved the most; to the one who had always loved him. It was a turning point, and Pinocchio began to acquire the virtues that would result eventually in his becoming a real boy.[19]

Today's gospel tells us a story that's in many ways like the story of Pinocchio and other folk tales like it, but crucially different from them all. In fact, those stories actually form a kind of backdrop to the gospel — a backdrop whose fabric is the predicament humanity has been in since the time of Adam and Eve — our repeated failure in the face of temptation.

The gospel tells us that there is a vast difference in the way Jesus deals with temptation and the way stories like *Pinocchio* show what the rest of us typically do. And it's a difference that brings to light what lies at the core of salvation.

Jesus is tempted by Satan to seize comfort, exercise dominion and revel in glory, but Jesus is no Pinocchio. Unlike Pinocchio, Jesus isn't interested in meeting Satan's expectations, and he certainly isn't counting on a Blue Fairy to show up and make it all nice.

What God wants to express, through his life on earth in Jesus, is quite another tale indeed, and Jesus refuses to have it be told any other way than his Father's way. It's a tale of courage, kindness, and selfless love that Jesus will relate to us in person as his life unfolds. It's the tale, which when you and I take it up into our own persons and live it out in word, Eucharist and action, that makes us God's children — the people you and I really are. And unlike the story of Pinocchio, it's not an earned privilege — it's a free gift that we simply have to accept and nurture with gratitude.

This is serious business — it is after all, possible to misunderstand the end game of evil and never become who we were really intended by God to be. Recall that the original story of Pinocchio did not have a happy ending.

There's a story like that — I'll warn you in advance it's kind of dark — about a man who was swept up in the events of World War II and gave in to the temptation to become a Nazi — partially out of fear for his life, but also partially out of a certain fascination with the power, prestige, and comfort the Nazis appeared to offer. But evil is intolerant to anything other than absolute submission to the lie however, and one day he rubbed the wrong person the

---

19 http://en.wikipedia.org/wiki/Pinocchio

wrong way and found himself seized in the middle of the night and taken away to a concentration camp.

Shocked at what he saw there, he approached a guard and demanded to see the commandant of the camp. The guard roared with laughter, decided to have some fun, and took him. The commandant could barely hold himself in and asked with mock seriousness how he could help.

The man looked straight at him and said, "There must be some mistake. I shouldn't be here. I'm innocent." It was only as he watched them laugh their ugly, gloating laugh, that it dawned upon him, as it had dawned upon little Pinocchio at various times in his story, that he wasn't innocent at all.

He had just simply and willingly been led along — and these people intended to destroy him — without remorse — without compunction. If not right then, soon enough, along with everyone else like him they could get their hands on.

He felt betrayed, used, and dirty. So indeed, he was, and he did not last very much longer, for you see, the end game of evil is always destruction. I wondered as I read that story why it was that sometimes people find it so hard to place their hope in God and so easy to trust in evil like that.

You and I can refuse to play the temptation game, as Jesus did, but it takes a different view of the world and a different view of who we are and what we're here for to be able to do that. Lent provides us an opportunity to embrace our destiny and get real.

Perhaps once upon a time, and maybe even now, you and I might have been only like pieces of wood — puppets in the hands of other people's expectations. Others who might not wish us well at all; who might even be laughing at us behind our backs as we lamely give in to the temptation to accept some evil or injustice, out of fear perhaps, or out of some illusory hope of personal advantage.

Enter into Lent with the rock-solid determination to become a child of God. Living the way Jesus shows us, we can indeed resist the temptation to be anything other than the tale that God would like to tell through our life and become real in the way our Father has always longed for us to be.

Questions For Discussion

1. Read *The Velveteen Rabbit* by Margery Williams. It can be viewed at no cost at this URL https://digital.library.upenn.edu/women/williams/rabbit/rabbit.html and then answer the question: "How do *I* become real?"
2. When has Pinocchio been a good metaphor to describe your life? When has it not?
3. Temptations are indeed morally neutral. Under what circumstances do they become dangerous? Lethal?

Your Worst Nightmare

Did you ever have one of those nightmares where company shows up at your house for the big dinner you've completely forgotten about? Or you dream that you're at work or in school stark naked and everyone's staring at you? Feels pretty good when you wake up and realize it was only a dream, doesn't it? If you've ever awakened from a nightmare like that, then you already know an awful lot about the meaning of today's gospel about the fig tree.

Although some commentaries interpret it as a call for us to shape up before God crushes us in our sins like bananas under a truck, a closer reading suggests that maybe the message is more an admonition to be ready than it is to shape up. Psalm 145 tells us that God is kind and full of compassion, slow to anger and abounding in love. A compassionate God doesn't watch over us with a stopwatch in one hand and a club in the other.

At the core of the message is the reality that in everyone's life there's a burning bush that needs to be approached. A surprising, remarkable manifestation of God's presence to which, like Moses, we're invited to draw near. Jesus tells us that to miss *that* invitation would indeed be our worst nightmare.

Let me tell you a little story. I used to teach statistics over at RPI. It was a lot of work, both for the students and for me. I'd encourage them to read the book and do their homework, but also to look at their jobs in the office or on the factory floor, keeping an eye out for something they can analyze for the statistics project they have to do. My aim was to have them change the way they thought about things so they could discover for themselves new ways to touch the underlying reality of what goes on in their daily lives.

One day, one of my students wandered into the classroom and was surprised when I asked him where his project was. He looked at me with horror and asked, "Was that due *today?*" Indeed, it had been.

Before I could say anything, one of the other folks said "Yeah, jerk — the way it says in the syllabus." The unexpressed judgment in the room as they all stared at this poor guy living his worst nightmare was, "We feel bad for you, man, but you messed up."

I could see that their understanding of reality was that although everyone has the right to be wrong, Mother Nature's judgment on error is death. Like the fig tree in the gospel, they expected me to cut this guy down.

As it turns out, I don't see things that way. To me, the whole point of teaching is about gently leading people to learn for themselves to see in new and richer ways, and to grow *into* that, free from anxieties about performance. I chatted with the young man offline later and we came up with an acceptable recovery plan that let him learn a thing or two about statistics, an awful lot about the value of being awake and aware of his responsibilities, and something about the quality of mercy.

Thinking about that student took me even deeper into the message of the gospel, and what repentance might mean. Remember how the folks whose blood Pilate mixed with their sacrifices were taken by surprise, kind of like my student? Remember those crushed by the falling tower who were also taken by surprise? No one expected that to happen.

When Jesus says that we might suffer a fate just like them, he's not talking about dying. That'll happen to everyone anyway, and death is imperfectly understood if it's seen simply as God's way of extracting vengeance.

What Jesus is talking about is being taken by surprise — being unready to meet our creator. Having never approached the burning bush of God's love and as a result, like the fig tree, never having borne the fruit we were created to bear, that's the nightmare, and it's the one from which Jesus urges us to awaken.

Remember the part of the gospel where there's a man who pleads with the owner of the fig tree to let it grow a bit longer? Some see Jesus in that story as the man who's pleading with his Father not to chop the fig tree down — with the fig tree standing for us, of course. But I wonder — do any of us really believe that God the Father's the bad cop and God the Son's the good cop like that?

The warning in this passage to repent or suffer the consequences is unmistakable, but maybe there are other ways we could think about it, too. Perhaps we could also imagine God as being the man who pleads with the owner of the orchard, and the owner as you and me; folks who can run out of patience pretty easily, all too ready sometimes, like a few of the folks in my class, to judge and cut one another down without mercy because someone doesn't meet our expectations or who is taking too long to shape up, in our not-so-humble opinion.

But God knows that the need is for care and cultivation, not destruction. The message to us is to lighten up as much as it is to shape up — there is neither need nor call for us to be each other's' worst nightmares.

It is, after all, what God does — for God's all about creation and growth, not destruction. His plea is for us not to cut each other down, but to accept his care and allow each other time to grow to become manifestations of God's love — branches on his burning bush, if you will.

Perhaps that's what God wishes to cultivate in us. It's the deeper meaning of repentance — that change of heart that opens us up to be transformed by the boundless, open-handed goodness of God and to be people through whom he can spread his love throughout our world.

It should come as no surprise then, that to repent and awaken to the reality of God's love means to awaken from the worst nightmare imaginable: a life lived unmindful of God.

Questions For Discussion

1. How would you describe your own "worst nightmare?"
2. Describe a time when you have experienced pure, unmerited, unexpected kindness? How did you feel?
3. Describe a time when you showed pure, unmerited, undeserved kindness to someone? Why did you do that? How did the experience make you feel?

Repentance

Artemus Ward, one of Mark Twain's friends is said to have remarked to him once "It ain't what we don't know that gets us into trouble. It's what we think we know that just ain't so."[20]

"Repentance" is one of those words we hear a lot, and many of us might think we know what it means pretty well. It's a translation of the Greek word *metanoia* which means to change one's mind. But what are we changing our minds about? Our behavior? Something else? That's where, for some of us, perhaps some of what we think we know about repentance just ain't so. Let me tell you a little story and you can decide if you agree.

My friend Ernie and his wife Frances, like many of us I'm sure, spent considerable time encouraging their children to keep their rooms clean. Early on it became apparent to them that the instruction "Go clean your rooms," was being interpreted by them as "go to your room and hide everything, especially the stuff you don't want us to find."

Ernie told me about one memorable day on which he and Frances told their son and two daughters to go clean their rooms, and then conducted a post-clean-up inspection. On the surface, everything was ship-shape, but their parents' sixth sense plus some unusual odors led Ernie and Frances to look around a bit more.

"That's when we found a petrified tuna fish sandwich, a full box of Cheerios, a dead frog, and my missing torque wrench all crammed between my son's bed and the wall," Ernie told me.

"Under our daughters' beds we discovered they'd found a home for three months' worth of dirty clothes, some of Meg's makeup that had gone missing, two full rolls of toilet paper, and a decomposing orange."

"In the discussion that followed," Ernie said, "we got some astonishing explanations of how all that stuff ended up where it did. Frances and I expressed muted admiration for their creative excuses, but then explained to them that there was a place for everything and that everything belonged in its place. Then we asked

20 https://quoteinvestigator.com/2018/11/18/know-trouble/ ,March 23, 2019

them why they'd hidden all those things like that. Did they really think all that stuff would never be discovered?"

"We were a little unhappy," Ernie continued sadly, "when they told us that they thought we'd judge them harshly if we found out what they'd done, especially since it was in direct violation of our family's frequently expressed rules about food, laundry, and other people's property. Frances and I told them we were a lot more disappointed that they hadn't simply admitted what they'd done and asked us for help getting things squared away again."

"Anger's not something you see much of in our household, even on a bad day; you know that Tim. If they'd done that, we said, they certainly wouldn't have been punished. Love, honesty and personal integrity, we told them, are much more important than flawless performance."

"But your children are amazing," I told Ernie. "It's hard for me to imagine they'd think you and Frances would've been harsh with them."

"Well, Tim," Ernie concluded, "we think they're pretty wonderful too, but at the time I'm not so sure they were convinced of how much leeway our love really afforded them, but we were able to get them to promise to try to change their ways. To their credit, they actually did change their ways over time. What made Frances and me the happiest though was when they told us they had come to believe that we really did love them very much and weren't going to hold them to some impossible standard of perfection."

Ernie's story helps illustrate what goes on with repentance and our relationship with God. At some level, all God wants us to do is keep our souls clean — not because it's convenient for God, but because it's good for us. Not only that, but God's perfectly willing and eager to help us.

On the surface our souls can look shiny clean, but appearances can be deceptive and underneath the veneer there may just be some stuff we've been hiding under the bed that we need to clean up; stuff that perhaps has some astonishing explanations about how it ended up hidden like that; stuff that God yearns for us to ask for help to clean up.

Sadly, many people keep the mess a big secret, so they think, although nothing's ever hidden from God. The reason for many is the same as what Ernie and Frances's children gave to them: they're afraid. Let's take a closer look.

The folks down at Baylor University have an ongoing study into attitudes about religion here in America.[21] The results give us insight into what drives our decision whether to hide or to repent. The first wave of the study revealed that roughly 40% of Catholics report that they believe in an angry, judgmental God.

Presumably they're not at all interested in giving God any reason to believe they've done anything out of line, for fear of being clobbered, and hiding looks like a pretty good strategy. A good first step for anyone who suffers in the grip of that belief would be to give yourself permission to change your mind about God's attitude toward you and your own attitude towards you as well. Remember, to repent means to change your mind.

In the gospel we just heard, Jesus invites us to repent and believe the good news. Think about it: an angry god wouldn't have much *good* news for anyone, would such a god? Maybe the yoke really is easy, and the burden quite light. As the psalmist writes in Psalm 145, "The Lord is kind and full of compassion, *slow* to anger and abounding in love...." Doesn't sound like an angry, judgmental God, does it? Preferring to focus on God's compassion rather than on our terror lets us begin to approach God with assurance of God's love, and confidence that we do in fact enjoy God's mercy.

The 60% of Catholics who happily accept the love of God as a matter of course might profitably come at repentance another way. Recently, Pope Francis wrote about the value of a daily examination of conscience, stating that it was the best way to keep alert to the things we're inclined to toss under our beds.

Few folks enjoy spending time thinking about how awful they are, but that's not what an examination of conscience is. Pope Francis explained that an examination of conscience is intended to be a thoughtful, honest and gentle time spent aware of being in the presence of God's unconditional love and acceptance.[22] We consider honestly what has brought us closer to God and what

21 https://www.baylor.edu/baylorreligionsurvey/doc.php/288937.pdf ,March 23, 2019
22 For example, https://www.americamagazine.org/content/dispatches/pope-francis-gives-roman-curia-15-point-examination-conscience March 23, 2019

has moved us further away, as individuals and in our relationships with other people. Although it's perfectly fine to grieve our moments of separation from God, that's light years away from despising ourselves for letting our rooms get messed up again.

A good examination of conscience embraces grateful acceptance of the good we've let God do through us, right along with acknowledgement of the good we've blocked through selfishness, malice or neglect. Indeed, if it weren't for the contrast, how could we appreciate the difference? The purpose of any examination of conscience is to situate ourselves in a place of open, vulnerable honesty with God so that we can gratefully accept God's mercy and love.

Questions For Discussion

1. What is your image of God? Upon what is that image based? How does that make you feel?
2. Why do people hide things, the way the children in the story did?
3. Is being without sin the same as perfection for us humans? Why or why not?

Trinity

Decades ago, I was asked by a Muslim co-worker named Saleh, or Sal, for short, to explain the Trinity. Sal wanted to know why we believed in three gods. I explained that we believe in just one, the same as he did. He objected, pointing out that we say we believe in the Father, the Son, and the Holy Spirit. That was three, as far as he could see.

I nodded, and then grabbed an old Boston Celtics patch I kept on my desk, offering to explain it to him through an analogy, the way St. Patrick used the shamrock to explain the Trinity to the Irish. He was okay with that, so I began by asking him some questions, to which I asked him simply to respond cheerfully, no matter how peculiar the question seemed. Being a good-natured sort as well as an excellent friend, he consented.

Then I asked him how many of himself there were. He laughed and said "One!" I agreed, laughing myself. Then I asked him if he was male or female. Once again, he laughed, and said "Tim — look at me; I'm a man!" I told him that was the answer I was hoping for, and we laughed together once more. Then I asked him how his lovely children were, and he said "Fine," and we talked about our delightful kids for a bit, the way happy dads do together.

Then I said, "Let me summarize where we've gotten so far, Sal. You've told me there's just one of you. Clearly, since you're a guy, you're someone's son. Beyond that, you've got kids, so you must be a father, too. In addition, you're Sal, my good friend — not my father or my son, just a happy spirit who loves and lets himself be loved by everyone and everything in God's good creation."

"This happy spirit of yours diffuses throughout your fatherhood, your sonship and your daily life as yourself here with me, right?" He modestly agreed that this was accurate. "And these aren't just 'roles,' Sal, the way our job titles are, yes?" He agreed to that, too; being a father and a son and being himself was indeed who he was.

Then I asked: "Sal, is there a time nowadays when you're not a father?"

"No," he replied.

"Is there a time when you're not a son?" I asked.

"How could that be?" He said.

"And is there a time when you're not yourself?" I continued.

He laughed, but then got quiet and stared at me intently, because he could see where I was going with all this. I asked one more question: "Sal, is everything you have as a father also exactly what you have as a son and also totally what you have as you yourself?" Sal agreed it would be irrational to think otherwise.

"My point's this, Sal," I said "You and I are analogies to the Trinity, not unlike Saint Patrick's shamrock is too, and it's not much different for women. We aren't God, but there's no time when we're not, in one being, three different persons, three different missions, if you will — fathers, sons, and ourselves or mothers, daughters, and ourselves. A parent's mission is different than a child's and they're both different from what it is to be your independent self, but they're all about love, wouldn't you say?" He nodded thoughtfully, rubbing his chin.

"It's similar to, but not identical to the way which we speak of God as love, and the persons of the Trinity being consubstantial, yet distinct persons, Sal. There are pretty big differences, too. For example, there's no way I can become something different, like a dog and save them all from something, the way the son became human in the incarnation and saved us, and I sure can't share myself with everyone, body and blood, soul and divinity, the way Jesus does in the Eucharist under the appearance of bread and wine." Sal agreed that would be quite alarming.

I concluded by telling him, "All this is just an analogy, Sal, not any kind of profound theology. My purpose isn't to explain the inner nature of God, but to show that our belief in the Trinity is by no means unreasonable. It's a belief that tells us something deeply significant about ourselves.

Who we are and how our ordinary, daily lives unfold mirrors the interior life of the Trinity. God indeed is the source of our being, and each of us is created in the image and likeness of God in any number of very recognizable ways. Saint Catherine of Genoa was on to something profound when she exclaimed, "My deepest me is God!"

Sal may still a be Muslim, as far as I know, but I remember

that he thanked me warmly and said no one had ever explained the Trinity to him quite like that. Who knows where God may have led him afterward? Perhaps it'll never happen to you, but then again, you never know when God might put someone in your path who'd like you to explain the Trinity to him or her. You might even be pretty astonished at who it is who's asking you. At that moment it would be enormously helpful for you to have a shamrock on hand and a story to tell.

Questions For Discussion

1. How would you explain the Trinity to a non-believer?
2. In what other ways can you discern the Trinitarian reality within yourself?
3. Consider the gift of God's self-revelation to you. How might you get in touch with this gift in prayer?
4. Take a look at Centering Prayer.[23] It is not the same as contemplative prayer, but it complements *lectio divina* very nicely and can dispose you for the gift of contemplative prayer in remarkable ways!

---

23   https://www.contemplativeoutreach.org/sites/default/files/private/method_cp_eng-2016-06_0.pdf, June 16, 2019

Hide And Seek

Not too long ago, my cousins, my brother and I were reminiscing about the games we used to play as children. Like most folks, we played a lot of hide-and-seek. One of my cousins remarked that she hated the game because no one ever came to look for her. We told her we *had* looked for her, but she always hid so well that we could never find her. At first, she glowed with pride, but then frowned and asked, "Wait a minute. Are you telling me the truth?"

"Of course we are!" We all lied, trying to look indignant.

It's a bit like that with God and us, too. We humans have been playing hide-and-seek with God since the time of Adam and Eve. Sometimes, when life's not going so well, it feels like God's hiding from us. At other times it's us trying to hide from God. Let's take a look at both sides of this coin which, curiously, really has only one side.

From time to time at the hospital, I meet with people in difficult situations. One older man in palliative care plaintively asked me once why he was still around. He was a wonderful guy, with solid faith, it seemed to me. He just couldn't find God anywhere in what seemed to be this pointless lingering. I suggested to him that maybe his problem was similar to the way it is in hide-and-seek: you're not looking in the right place.

He asked me what I meant, and I told him that he might still be here so that he could show the rest of us how to die with grace and dignity. None of us had anything resembling his experience of dying, so how could *we* possibly know? We needed him to show us how. God was very much present within him, ready to teach us that lesson if he would allow God to do that through him. Nope, God wasn't playing hide-and-seek with him at all.

If he needed a clue, I said, the Eucharist provides a big hint. I pointed to a host in the pyx I was carrying and said, "Look—there's the body, blood, soul, and divinity of Jesus Christ, hidden right in front of us, in the appearance of bread and wine. To receive the Eucharist is to engage in a game of hide-and-seek like none we've ever played before, and nobody ever stays lost."

He nodded as I spoke and then told me he'd been a catechist and a small Christian community leader at his parish. "All those years I taught people how to live in Christ," he mused. "Maybe, as you suggest, God's asking me now to show people how to die in Christ." No wonder I couldn't find him. He was hidden in a place I didn't think I wanted to go."

I gently encouraged him to think about it. Then I gave him Communion and went away quietly. He died a few days later. The nurses told me he spent his last days cheerfully telling everyone who came into his room that he loved them and was very grateful for their care. Everyone had been deeply touched; they could tell it came from his heart. He had found God in his situation, and God had found him.

Sometimes it's us who're doing the hiding. As we grow out of childhood, the rules and context of hide-and-seek change, and the game becomes more complex. Some grow up hiding from their true feelings, some heart-breakingly hide from those who love them, others hide criminal behavior and myriad kinds of betrayals large and small.

In a word, we choose to sin. We know where to find God, but we don't go looking for him any more than my brother and I really went looking for our cousin during our hide-and-seek games. At root, all sin is hiding from reality and the love that drew it forth into being. It's a refusal to find God, who is actually never hiding. It may come as a surprise to find out who's really doing all the hiding. Saint Catherine of Genoa used to say that her deepest self was God. As it turns out, when we hide from God, it's not God we're hiding from, but our truest, most authentic selves, who live and move and have our being in God.

We may refuse to look for God, but as scripture tells us, God continues to look for us until we find out true selves in him. Let me tell you another story.

From time to time, I meet with a group of Catholic recovering alcoholics, as their chaplain. Alcoholics are masters of the art of hide-and-seek. One day, one of the folks, let's call him Bill, told me his tale of hitting rock bottom.

"I thought I could stop drinking any time I wanted," Bill said. "The problem was that I could also start again any time I wanted to. My whole life was all about me. I made up my own private world the way I wanted it to be. I could glimpse the unreality of it every so often, but it never hit home until I lost everything, and almost my life. I remember exactly the moment I decided to get help."

"What happened?" I asked.

"Someone had suggested I go on a Matt Talbot retreat, just to see what 'those kind of people' did. At first, I resisted because I knew I wasn't like 'those kind of people' at all. But my friend persisted, and I went. In one of the talks, the priest asked 'How much longer are you going to play hide-and-seek? Hide-and-seek with God. Hide-and-seek with the rest of us and all creation. Hide-and-seek with yourself.' In that moment I realized that's what I had been doing. I thought God had been hiding from me and didn't want to be found. I saw in a flash that it was me who was doing all the hiding. I *was* one of 'those kind of people'. I don't play hide-and-seek anymore, Tim," Bill told me. "Now I find God hidden everywhere! Even in me. Even in you."

So, when God seems to be playing hide-and seek with you, or vice versa, take a hint from Bill and look around. Still can't find him? Might be time to stop hiding and celebrate the sacraments of reconciliation and Eucharist. Those, it seems, are God's favorite hiding places.

Questions For Discussion

1. What games of "hide-and-seek" have you played in your life, if any?
2. Have you ever felt that God isn't interested in "finding" you? What is that like?
3. How do you respond to those in your experience who appear to be playing the hiding game?

Unclean

Jesus is a healer, one who has power over life and death. As such, he's far more concerned about alleviating human suffering than he is about technical legalisms concerning what's clean or unclean.

Clean, to the Jewish folks of his time, meant that you could show up in public, touch and converse with other people, and worship. Unclean meant that you'd better keep to yourself for a while, stay away from us and take the prescribed paths to straighten yourself out. Cleanliness rules were a way to order society, decide who's one of us and who's not, who's in and who's out. It seems it was a major preoccupation of the time. Over two thirds of the written material we have from the Pharisaic tradition of Jesus' time dealt with matters of cultic purity.[24]

At the time Mark was writing his gospel, his audience of Jewish and Gentile converts were uneasy with one another, mainly because of the difference in importance that they placed on Jewish ritual purity. By placing a hemorrhaging woman in the middle of a crowd and having Jesus touch a dead girl, both of which would've jumped out at the Jewish converts as being horrific examples of the unclean, Mark makes it clear in his gospel that purity concerns don't matter a bit to Jesus, but relief of human suffering does.

Jesus, it would seem, wants to show us that God's mercy is far more important than observance of cultic rules. Contrary to the dynamic of ritual purity, that mercy is inclusive rather than exclusive. It defines all of us as "in," and nobody as "out". That is one of the deepest meanings of our identity as a Eucharistic community.

If there's any requirement at all, it isn't about cleanliness, but rather that we simply have the courage to approach Jesus with confidence, ask for and then accept the healing he freely offers. There are no gospel narratives that describe Jesus saying anything like, "Oh look, some dead people. Let me shake folks up a bit, go over there and raise a few of them to life." Nope, it seems we have to have the courage and humility to take the initiative.

---

24 http://nd.edu/~jneyrey1/purity.html, June 26, 2012

Having to ask implies that we acknowledge that something's not right with us, believe that Jesus can get our wheels back on the road, ask, and then receive what we need with gratitude. It sounds simple, but it's not. It would seem that not too many of us are willing to admit there's a funny noise coming from under our hood. That would make us unclean, in our own minds — unworthy to be out in public unsupervised, unworthy to be around anyone else, let alone approach God.

Perhaps there are cleanliness rules of our own that prevent us from experiencing God's mercy and sharing it with others. What are our honest feelings about our own real or imagined shortcomings? Are we, in our own opinions, "in" or "out"? Clean or unclean? How about people of other religions, folks with same-sex attraction, immigrants, the poor and homeless, or even just quiet folks and loud people? Are they "in" or "out" to us? Clean or unclean?

Let me tell you a story about someone who was convinced she was "out." A few months ago, I was on volunteer duty over at the hospital when a call came in the little hours of the morning from the NICU — the neonatal intensive care unit. These are usually heartbreakers, in which a child or a mom has died, but when I called it turned out that mother and child were both alive and well — mom just wanted to talk. I was relieved about that and made my way down to the NICU.

I found mom resting alone in her bed, waiting to be taken to see her baby, who was tiny and under close observation elsewhere. As we began to chat, she told me that she was sad. I asked her if she wanted to tell me about that, and she told me a tale that contained equal parts of unbelievable oppression and self-loathing.

She'd had a number of children already and hadn't graduated from high school, as her childhood friends had. Her husband didn't have a good job, and money was tight. They were living with his parents, and they were not particularly supportive. She felt like a failure and wondered if her life would ever get any better.

I reflected the question back to her and she said it would take a miracle. I asked her if she prayed for that.

"Miracles never happen," she said.

"You just gave birth to one," I replied.

She stopped for a moment to think about that, and I added "You're a miracle, too, you know. There has never been anyone like you and never will be again. In God's eyes you're precious beyond belief."

"Maybe God thinks so," she replied, "but my in-laws don't. They hate me. I don't feel like part of their family at all."

In that moment thoughts of cleanliness and uncleanliness spun through my head. This young mom wasn't experiencing God's love and mercy from within or from without. She was suffering in a web of judgment as terrible as the woman's suffering in our gospel story today. Like Jairus' daughter, she was in a very real sense quite dead.

"You're part of God's family," I told her. "It's a vast family of love and no one can exclude you from that. There's nothing you can say or do, or not say or not do that would separate you from it. Widen your eyes and consider all the lovely people here who are taking care of you and your baby. You matter to us."

Our conversation went on for a while, maybe forty minutes or an hour. She gradually became more relaxed and peaceful. A nurse came in eventually to take her off to see her baby, and as I left, I smiled at her and thanked her for the miracle of bringing another beautiful little person into our world.

"Maybe other miracles will happen to me now, too," she said, smiling back. I do hope so. There's no way of knowing how things went for her after she went home with her baby, but that's God's lookout now, it seems to me. All that was required of me or anyone like me in that moment was to allow God to show God's love and mercy to a person desperately in need of it, to raise her from that death in life we can suffer when we're feeling oppressed and unloved.

It's like that for all of us in our everyday dealings, too. The challenge to us all is to allow God to extend mercy and love to us and through us. You'll be aware that it's happening because you'll find yourself more often encouraging rather than critical, compassionate rather than contemptuous and inclusive in love rather than exclusive. You may even find God's power going out from you from time to time without you even being aware that anyone touched you.

I know I'm only so-so with all that myself, but I also know I'm a work in progress.

It's so important to keep working at it, and never give up, for the last person we'd ever want to be convinced is irretrievably unclean is ourselves.

Questions For Discussion

1. In the event you happen to have them, who's on your "clean" and" unclean" lists?
2. What's it like for you when you're feeling unclean, unloved and oppressed?

Ray

What follows is the funeral homily I was privileged to offer at the funeral of our good friend Ray. I hope we all get to encounter someone like Ray and his lovely wife Agnes in our lives. Read on and see why...

Many people don't know this, but when a new soul is created, it gets paired up with an old soul, and the two of them travel to the earth to look around for a while so that the new soul can see if it wants to go through with life or not. So it happened that one day a while ago, a baby soul got paired up with an old soul and off they went to the earth to see what it was like.

It didn't go all that well at first. The baby soul was horrified at how poorly some people treated others, how some families just didn't get along, and how many people were just so loud and selfish and mean-spirited. The baby soul looked up at the old soul and said:

"Let's get out of here! This place is out of control. Everyone hates each other and no one cares."

The old soul said, "Maybe you're making too quick a judgment, baby soul. May I show you something special?"

The baby soul wasn't so sure. "It had better be good," it said.

Then the old soul took them both to Ray and Ag's place.

"Let's stay here for a while, baby soul. Maybe when you see what they're like, you'll change your mind. Start by watching Ray for a bit and let me know what you think."

So, the baby soul watched Ray at work and saw how he went about things.

"He treats people well," the baby soul said to the old soul. "He doesn't scream like the others, cut corners, lie or put people down."

"No, baby soul," the old soul said, "he doesn't. That's Ray for you."

"He gets along with people and treats them with patience, kindness and respect!" the baby soul said.

"Yes, baby soul," the old soul said, "he does. That's Ray for you."

Then the baby soul followed Ray home and watched some more.

"Wow!" the baby soul said, "He really loves his wife, doesn't he?"

"I'll say," the old soul agreed, "they're like two peas in a pod. Can't tell who takes better care of whom."

The baby soul sat around for some time, and watched as family and friends called up, dropped by, or celebrated birthdays, graduations and anniversaries together.

" Look at them!" the baby soul exclaimed. "They love each other. This sure isn't like what I saw when I first came down here."

"No, baby soul, it isn't," the old soul said, "There's a reason for that, as you'll see presently. This family is something above and beyond, and that Ray — well he's something truly special."

"How special?" the baby soul asked.

The old soul played with space-time the way old souls can do when they're on assignment and showed the baby soul Ray busy with his snow-blower, plowing his neighbors' sidewalk.

"Who's that?" the baby soul asked.

"Just call him Dugo," the old soul said, "don't try to pronounce his real name."

"Did he ask Ray to do that for him?" the baby soul asked.

"Nope," the old soul said. "Ray just does that without being asked."

"He pays him, doesn't he?" the baby soul asked.

The old soul just laughed and said "No way! Even if he tried, Ray wouldn't take a dime."

"Why does he do that?" the baby soul asked.

"He loves people, baby soul," the old soul said. "And it's not just Dugo. Ray's that way with everyone. He cares about folks."

The baby soul took that in and then said:

"But he's not talking with anyone, he's just doing work for them. He's probably just one of those quiet guys who likes to stay under the radar."

"Umm... not really, baby soul. Just a minute," the old soul said and rewound space-time to the day before Thanksgiving.

"Who's that guy?" the baby soul asked when the spinning stopped.

"That's his son, Ray Jr.," the old soul said.

"Why does he look so frustrated?" the baby soul asked.

"He's trying to phone Ray Sr., but he can't get through," the old soul said.

"Why not?" the baby soul asked.

"Ray Sr.'s calling everyone he ever knew to chat for a bit, catch up on what's been going on, and wish everyone a happy Thanksgiving."

"Everyone?" the baby soul asked.

"Yes," the old soul said. "Everyone. Here, Italy; doesn't matter where folks are. If they're in his heart, they'll be getting a call. Ray Jr. won't be able to get through until tomorrow, if he's lucky. He's been doing this seems like forever. Ray Jr. likes to say that Ray Sr. came up with Facebook before it was even invented."

"What's Facebook?" the baby soul asked.

"You'll find out after you're born," the old soul said.

"I'm still not sure I want to come here, old soul," the baby soul said. "This Ray friend of yours works well with others, seems to treat his wife and family pretty well, helps other folks and calls them up, but what's he like face to face with his friends?"

"Well, baby soul," the old soul said, "to understand that you have to understand about this first [hold up Ray's big wine bottle]. You know, it's one thing to wish a person happy a whatever over the phone, but quite another to share a bit of good cheer face to face. See how worn out this spigot is?"

"Looks like he shared an awful lot of 'good cheer' with folks," the baby soul said.

"Oh, yes, that's what it looks like, baby soul," the old soul said, "but Ray never overdid it. Ray's deepest cheer really came from the love he had for his friends and family. He didn't need this stuff to make believe he loved and was loved."

"Where'd he learn to love like that?" the baby soul asked.

"It started with his family, folks like his brother, and lots of other people," the old soul said, "but the roots of his ability to love run deep."

"How deep?" the baby soul asked.

The old soul rewound his space-time gimmick one more time and they both found themselves here at Saint Pat — right over there someplace. The baby soul watched as Ray sang and distributed Communion to people.

"He looks just like,…" the baby soul started to say.

"Yes," the old soul said, finishing the sentence for the baby soul. "He looks just like the very person he's distributing to his fellow parishioners, doesn't he?"

"He does!" the baby soul said. "How'd he do that?"

"It's actually more that something's been done for him, baby soul," the old soul said. "He's just very much in tune with it. He did what was right, loved tenderly and walked humbly with the God who chose to love him unconditionally and share his very life with him. Ray figured out early on he wanted to be just like that, too."

The baby soul took that in and then turned to the old soul and said: "I know it's risky, but if I can be like Ray, if I can love and be loved like that, I think I'll go through this thing you call life."

"Sounds like a plan, baby soul," the old soul said. "Hold on to your faith, love and allow yourself to be loved deeply, and your life will be just as beautiful a thing as it was for Ray and everyone who knew him."

Questions For Discussion

1. How would you like to be remembered after you pass from this life?
2. Place yourself in the shoes of the "old soul" and tell others a story about someone exceptional you happen to know.

How To Listen To A Bad Homily

"Jesus Christ," you pray, "it's him again. Lord, give me strength." You certainly aren't the first one who has ever uttered that prayer, and likely not to be the last. It does beg the question though, of exactly what it is about the preacher's homily that has set your teeth on edge. Is it the homily, the homilist or perhaps something else? This chapter offers some thoughts to help you consider how you, personally, listen to a "bad" homily.

During formation we preachers are told that our first two years' worth of homilies should be discarded and never again see the sunlight, since we're just learning what to do and how to do it well. Like any exercise, there's no substitute for practice and repetition. But we all start out weak, and our earliest hearers, sad to say, are the ones whose destiny it is to die for the country. That bad homily you heard may just have been a priest, deacon or bishop cutting his teeth. There is, after all, such a thing as bad luck.

Destined to be newly assigned somewhere, we were told we'd all be starting from scratch, learning about the people in our parishes and other venues. Over time, we'd come to know their stories, their likes and dislikes, what holds their attention and what doesn't and other things like that. We'd develop some sense of comfort speaking in front of them. All in due time.

The probability of feeling supremely confident and knowing everything we need to on day one was zero. Given that, we were told that we could expect to hear both encouragement and criticism and to develop a sense of gratitude for both, but in particular, a thick skin for the latter.

The homily preachers preach and the homily people hear are rarely the same. One Sunday many years ago, when I was still a baby deacon, I was confronted after a mass at which I'd preached by a man who was not happy. "Every now and then you give a decent homily," he said, scowling. "Why can't you ever string a couple of them together?"

His wife, standing by, was mortified by her husband's behavior. As he continued to catalog my deficiencies, another man came up behind us who had not been privy to our conversation. "I'm just visiting here from California," he said to me as he passed by, in earshot of the complaining husband and his anxious wife. "We'll pay your airfare to come out and preach to us." That stopped the harangue dead in its tracks. The complainer's jaw dropped and his wife lit up with an ear-to-ear grin. "*De gustibus non est disputandum*," I quipped. "Guess there's no accounting for taste," I smiled disingenuously and eased the conversation to as cheerful a conclusion as we could manage.

The moral of that story is pretty clear: every homily isn't for everybody. Not enjoying what you're hearing? It may not be your day. Saint Ephrem the Syrian, a deacon of some renown and a doctor of the church, had something to say about that. He wrote that scripture itself strikes various readers differently at different times. What he said about reading scripture also goes for listening to homilies. Here's what he wrote, in his commentary upon the *Diatesseron*:

"Lord, who can comprehend even one of your words? We lose more of it than we grasp, like those who drink from a living spring. For God's work offers different facets according to the capacity of the listener, and the Lord has portrayed his message in many colors, so that whoever gazes upon it can see in it what suits him. Within it he has buried manifold treasures, so that each of us might grow rich in seeking them out…."[25]

It may still strike you that some of the treasure's buried pretty deep. Indeed, more can go wrong in preparing a homily than in preparing your grandmother's bananas supreme. Let's take a look and consider appropriate responses.

What Can Go Wrong…

- It's too long. The green zone timing in our neck of the woods looks like this:
    - Weekdays 1-3 minutes
    - Sundays 5-6 minutes

To calculate the yellow zone, add thirty seconds to each of the above. Beyond that a homilist is asking for, and deserves, trouble.

25 http://www.liturgies.net/Liturgies/Catholic/loh/week6sundayor.htm, February 18, 2019

- It's too short. Consider the following dialogue, heard after mass one day:
    "What'd he talk about?"
    "He never said."

- Aristotle's *Poetics* is a good, short read that can help. It points out the obvious: all homilies should have a beginning, a middle and an end. Tell them what you're going to tell them, tell them, and then tell them what you told them. If you're listening to a homily that violates this principle, do what actors do with ellipses (those dots […] you see in playscripts and other literature). Make something up in the moment that's not in the script but sounds like something that would fit in the homily pretty well. In plays, it makes the ellipses work. It can do the same for homilies, but it requires you to provide the artwork.

- It's too diffuse. Homilies should have one theme. One. Just one. Really, only one. Never more than one. If it doesn't, pick one from your bouquet and let the rest go.

- I've heard all this before. Perhaps you have. Perhaps the person next to you hasn't. Time to pray for the homilist and for those to whom this message is brand new. Remember, this week's homily might not be directed at you. At a subtler level, you may have fallen into the trap of "I know you think you understand what you thought I said but I'm not sure you realize that what you heard is not what I meant," sometimes attributed to Alan Greenspan[26], and for good reason. As a homilist, I'm sometimes flabbergasted at what people have told me they thought I'd said. A brief exchange usually clears things up, except when people have chosen to be offended. Grant the homilist the possibility that you mightn't have understood the homily as he meant it to be understood, talk it over and let there then be peace on earth.

- It's incomprehensible. What? You don't understand the apokatathesic hermeneutic? Transubstantiation got you bewildered? There's really no hope here. The homilist is in his own world, and the reason he's there likely isn't pretty. Try private

---

26 https://www.goodreads.com/quotes/204034-i-know-you-think-you-understand-what-you-thought, August 20, 2019

prayer for a bit. You can pray for the homilist's soul. Afterwards, say something in a foreign language to the homilist and ask him what he thinks. Consider a bright quip in Hindi, perhaps something along the lines of यह समझ से बाहर था.[27]

- If it's incomprehensible because the preacher's native language isn't yours, try translating what he's saying into another language, preferably one you don't know very well. This will give you a sense of what the preacher's up against, and perhaps evoke a compassionate response within your heart. That's as good an outcome as any homily can hope to deliver anyway, so be happy with that.

- The homilist can't pronounce things properly, such as, the way *I* do, for example, "Ay-men" rather than "Ah-men," the way Jesus (and Barabbas) did.

    On the other hand, the homily you're hearing may be astonishing. Let's take a look at that also and prevent a good homily from becoming a bad one in your mind.

What Can Go Right

- The message today is spot on for you. Don't deny it just because it's *him*. Embrace it, put it in your own words, pray about it and talk it over with folks.

- The message wasn't for you today, but you know someone on whose foot this shoe belongs. Figure out how you can gently present it to this person in a way that will really help him or her. This is facilitated by those homilists who generously post their homilies online someplace for those with hearing difficulties, for those for whom English is a foreign language, and for those who need non-reputable documentation when they write to complain to the bishop.

- The homilist has cleaned up his act. Encourage him by complimenting him.

- Something in the homily triggered a really significant, unrelated movement within you. Don't let this one get away — discern whether it's the Holy Spirit (such as, is it loving, true,

27 "That was incomprehensible" — phonetically: "yeh samajh sey bahar tha"

helpful, inspiring, necessary, kind, peaceful, challenging…) and ponder it in your heart, the way Mary did.

- The homily presented something that piqued your curiosity. Some churches provide paper and pencils for you to scribble down a word or two to help you remember what it was later on. Even if the homilist got it wrong, he made you look.
- The homily challenged a strongly held opinion of yours. This will make you angry, more than likely, but don't throw the baby out with the bathwater. Explore the reasons you became angry. There's apt to be some treasure buried there, as Saint Ephrem would say.
- The homilist is clearly in command of the teaching of the US Catholic bishops about how to prepare a homily.[28] If he mentioned love, Jesus, and the Eucharist there has *got* to be something in there worth a listen!

What Can I Do?

Since it's usually not possible to control who's giving the homily, here are some additional tips that can help, whether you're enamored of the homilist or not:

1. Prepare yourself. If you've read the readings, you likely know what's in them and can be prepared to listen with discernment and fill in the blanks. Sometimes there's great value to be had comparing your understanding of scripture and the homilist's.
2. Observe what's being said, but decide not to criticize. Here's the difference:
   a. Observation: "I'm not sure I agree with him about that."
   b. Criticism: "If brains were dynamite, this idiot couldn't blow his nose."
   This advice works well in other venues, too.
3. Give them the benefit of the doubt. Maybe they know something you don't. You might even have been wrong about

[28] http://www.usccb.org/beliefs-and-teachings/vocations/priesthood/priestly-life-and-ministry/upload/usccb-preaching-document.pdf, June 9, 2019

something. No matter what, he's doing the best he can. You'd appreciate the same consideration.

4. Remember that the message may not be for you today.
5. If you are getting upset, imagine the preacher with an elephant snout. No, really! It's an old technique that can cure dyspepsia almost immediately. Remember not to burst out in laughter, if you feel that coming on. You'd have to explain....
6. Close your eyes and imagine someone else is delivering the homily. Start with General George Patton and work your way up through the inventory to Jesus. The person whose voice you choose has something to say to you. Why did you choose *that* voice?
7. Look over the shoulder of your discomfort and try to discern what's motivating your response. Are you projecting something onto the homilist? Perhaps transferring some hostility, you feel towards someone else (maybe even yourself) onto him? If so, you're just being human, but it's wise to admit that to yourself.
8. It may just be that against your deepest inclination you're actually *enjoying* the homily this time, even though it's *him*. Let that happen and try to remember a line or two that you can use yourself later on. Wrestle a bit with that inclination not to listen, but don't judge anyone, especially yourself.
9. Form some words you can share with the homilist later on, such as, "I can't find enough good things to say about your homily today," "You never cease to amaze me with what you say." Of course, sometimes just "thanks" will do.
10. Take a hint from Evagrius Ponticus, one of the Desert Fathers, and take a seven deadly sins sanity check on yourself, and the homilist. The seven deadlies are pride, envy, anger, sloth, avarice, gluttony, and lust. Evagrius speaks of these as inclinations to sin, rather than as explicit sins in themselves.

Are we *proud* today? You are, if you think you're better than the homilist or anyone else in the congregation. What's with that, hmm? Watch out for the "smartest guy in the room" effect. There really is exactly only one such creature, it's true. In your mind you may have established that it isn't the homilist. Modesty would suggest that it probably isn't you, either.

Perhaps you're *envious* — "It should be *me* up there, not *him*. I'd tell these people something they'd never forget." But you're not the deacon, priest, bishop, abbot, abbess or pope, so name your envy, deal with it, and be happy being who you are instead of wishing you were someone you're not. Chances are you would indeed be unforgettable, but probably not the way you think.

Angry? Most, if not all anger stems from frustration of some sort. No one can *make* you angry — you have to allow something to get to you. Anger *per se* is not a sin, nor even necessarily an inclination to one. Wrath is though, since it leads to grudges, resentments and eventually enemies, if left unaddressed. If you feel angry, it's time to do that "looking over the shoulder" thing.

The last four deadlies are likely less common phenomena in the universe of homily responses — you can decide for yourself if they're in the mix somehow. Evagrius simply recommends that we identify them honestly (it's okay to feel them), but then look behind the inclination and ask what's motivating it. That's where the sin always is, and that's where you may find the root of your discomfort with the homily.

Allow the homily to affect you as best you can. If you're human, some days you'll simply be closed for business. For all the people who have complained about the homilies I've given, there have been far more who've either told me they enjoyed listening, and in some cases, gripped my hand and told me I'd saved their lives. Honest. That shouldn't be too surprising, for in the final analysis, everything that goes on at mass has to do with life and love.

I shall conclude with a tale of one of the Desert Fathers[29] who was approached by a monk who could simply not stand one of the priests in the monastery. The Desert Father listened attentively as the monk railed against the priest's irreverence, stupidity, inability to preach and so forth. When he had finished, the Desert Father asked him: "If you were thirsting to death in the desert and a leper offered you a glass of water, would you take it?" The

---

29   Benedicta Ward, SLG, *The Sayings of the Desert Fathers*, Cistercian Publications, 1975.

monk listened, nodded with understanding, then rose, thanked the Desert Father and left.

I can imagine that after he left, he returned to his church and calmly endured the priest he could not stand. Looking about him, understanding that he didn't understand how God was mysteriously working in anyone in that exact moment, let alone himself, he perhaps smiled and prayed: "Jesus Christ, it's you again, isn't it?"

Questions For Discussion

1. Consider a memorable homily or two that you've experienced. How did the good ones affect you? How did the bad ones make you feel?

2. What *one* piece of advice would you give to homilists? Why did you pick that one?

3. One of the most fabulous compliments I've ever been given was from a person who simply looked at me, shook my hand and told me "You're the real deal." In the end, is it the homily, the homilist, or something else altogether that makes for a good homily?

The First Eucharist Quiz

1. The word "Eucharist" is derived from a Greek word that means:

    a. Communion

    b. Thanksgiving

    c. Peace

    d. Reconciliation

2. After consecration, the host we receive is truly the body, _____, _____ and _____ of Jesus Christ.

3. During Eucharistic Adoration devotions, the host is displayed in a:

    a. Thurible

    b. Monstrance

    c. Sacrarium

    d. Anabasis

4. The Eucharistic miracles witnessed over the centuries consistently show Jesus' blood type to be:

    a. A

    b. A+

    c. O

    d. AB

5. The cup which holds the wine that becomes the blood of Jesus through the action of the priest is called a:

    a. Ciborium

    b. Chalice

    c. Paten

    d. Radix

6. All 33,000 +/- Christian denominations believe exactly what Catholics do concerning the Eucharist.

   a. True

   b. False

7. Divorced people may not receive Holy Communion.

   a. True

   b. False

8. The last Eucharist we receive in this life is called:

   a. Viaticum

   b. Exeunt omnia

   c. Sayonara extremis

   d. Non sequitur

9. For valid medical reasons, a priest may substitute another liquid for the wine used in Eucharistic celebrations.

   a. True

   b. False

10. Hosts not distributed during mass are stored in the:

    a. Tabernacle

    b. Lumen gentium

    c. Uvula

    d. Solarium

This quiz is used as a conversation-starter in meetings with the parents of children receiving their First Eucharist. The purpose is to teach and clarify — please use it as you see fit, but we encourage you to choose not to use it as a club or a means to humiliate people. We let people work together on the answers if they like — you decide what's best for you. Depending upon your audience, you may find yourself not so much catechizing as evangelizing!

Tips on how to use the quiz:

1. Very gently, with compassion and good humor
2. Have a prize — consider a loaf of bread and a bottle of wine. There is, just for the record, a brand of red wine called *Our Daily Red*.
3. This quiz is about a lot more than the Eucharist. You have an opportunity to go deep with people and we encourage you to do just that. Here are just a few thoughts about how you might wish to follow up with each question:

    a. *Eucharist* does mean "Thanksgiving." Thanks, and praise are the foundation of Christian prayer. In our RCIA groups, the first prayer we teach people is "Thanks!" It begins to wean them away from themselves as the center of the universe, among other things. The second prayer is 'Wow!" and the third is "Love you!" placed on a Post-It™ note placed on their bathroom mirror. Everything we do as Catholics connects to the Eucharist, and these three simple prayers go a long way towards making that connection simple, explicit and joyful.

    b. "Blood," "Soul" and "Divinity" go in the blanks. We like to explain that bodies are presence. If your body isn't here, you are not present, are you? So, the Eucharist is the presence of Jesus Christ. Likewise, if you have no blood, you are dead. So, blood therefore means the life of Jesus Christ. Soul is explained as our real identity in the presence of God — far more than a story or a philosophical explanation. The ground of what's real is being shared with you by that ground himself. Divinity is easily grasped as "everything," although you may have to shape that thought a bit for people.

    c. A monstrance is used for Adoration. The word, in English, dates from the fifteenth century and comes from the Latin *monstrare*, which simply means "to show."

    d. Jesus' blood type, according to the various sources that describe it, is AB. The Universal Receiver. Indeed, what else could it be? Something to ponder.

e. Most folks know what the chalice is. Usage of the word in English dates from the fourteenth century. It simply means "cup," from the Latin *calix*.

f. Please tell people that divorced Catholic people may continue to receive the Eucharist. Divorced Catholics remarried without benefit of annulment need to chat with their pastor, who will advise them properly about what to do.

g. The Eucharist lies at the heart of Roman Catholicism and its cousins. We thankfully receive the gift of himself that Jesus Christ offers us. You can show people a crucifix at this point and tell them that as far as you know, the crucifix is the only religious symbol in the world that has a person at the center of it. There's a reason for that.

h. Viaticum is the last Eucharist a person receives in this life. The word, in English, dates from the fourteenth century and comes from the Latin *viaticus*, which means "journey."

i. Nope — it has to be wine. Maybe wine with only an itsy-bitsy amount of alcohol in it, but you can't use beer, soda or anything else that's not wine.

j. "Tabernacle" comes from the Latin *tabernaculum* and dates from the thirteenth century, in English. It means "tent" or "hut." The hut Jesus Christ loves best is your heart and mine.

Questions For Discussion

1. How'd you do? How does your "score" make you feel? (Please remember that there really isn't any "score").

2. How might you use this quiz with your family, friends, co-religionists and folks of other faith traditions?

Poems

The poems in this section have not come from homilies. Rather, they've emerged from reflection upon different experiences that have touched me in some way deeper than everyday experiences. When I look at them, they all do have a message, which is not surprising to me given the way my mind works.

Apologies in advance for any that contain imagery you may find gross, but that's simply the way the thing came out and, by the way, Jesus himself spoke too, without apology, of that which passes out of the body (Matthew 15:17)!

Weeding

This weed's shallow;
Not like that one over there,
That goes to the center of the earth.

This one sprawls its unpleasant self,
Like your lazy kid lacking job and purpose,
Who's decided to move back in.

This one's actually pretty,
With its small yellow flowers delicately
Choking my tomatoes to death.

Over here's the invasive jihad
Challenging established eggplants
And threatening peppers with doom.

I can only rip their heads off,
As surely they would mine,
For weeds and I share disdain for mercy.

I pull;
They're back.
I pull;
They're back.

I can no more free my garden of them,
Than I can free my mind of you,
Whose roots run deep within me,
Sprawling uninvited,
Seeking endless death,
Worse than mere extinction.

But winter ends the weeding.
Winter, when nothing grows,
Except the growing feeling
That the weeds and their seeds
Are making plans.

Questions For Discussion

1. What's this poem really about?
2. Where are the "weeds" in your life?

Take a moment to consider what the poem says about "faith" and "hope," even though those terms aren't explicitly used.

Pain

It's just you and me.
The world around us vanished,
The hour you arrived.

Relentless,
You slice my days and nights;
Cut after cut after cut....

You demand attention unchallenged;
I receive nothing in return.

Bellowing lest I sleep,
You grip me by the neck,
Whispering despair in both my ears.

You sever me from thought and song;
You suck me into your shadow.

The touch of my beloved,
Disfigured by your evil chemistry,
Rips my skin like a claw;

With an evil laugh you gloat,
For well you know,
Until you leave without farewell,
It'll be just you and me.

Questions For Discussion

1. What is pain? Is it the same thing as suffering?
2. Reflect on painful times in your own life. Does the poem reflect any thoughts or feelings you may have had in that time?

Midnight In My Daughter's Old Room

Moonlight in your empty room
Dimly reveals your bookcase.

The stories I'd read to you
As vague to me now
As the bookcase itself.

Your bed still smells of you.
Pooh-bear leans on your pillow,
As if to whisper dream-talk,
But your head now rests
On another pillow, somewhere else.

This empty room,
So full of silence,
So full of words unspoken....
Saturated with dreams,
The silence curls about me like warm, wet summer air
On still and moonless nights.

Were there words unsaid?
Gestures withheld?
What is this loneliness I feel for you, and me;
This terrible longing?

I ache and wonder,
Did you love me?
Did you know how much I loved you?

Who tells you stories now?
Whose fingers touch your cheek,
Resting on that pillow somewhere else.

Unanswered, the questions
Sink into darkness,
Like the memory of all
Those stories I'd read to you.

I leave your room,
That empty, sacred space,
Blessed now by moonlight
And tears.

Questions For Discussion

1. What are the sacred spaces in your own life?
2. The poet is describing an ache of some sort. What do you think it is?
3. As your life unfolds, how are you handling regrets, missed opportunities and failures?

Landing Soon

The plane lurches,
Its sudden deceleration
Feeling like a missed heartbeat;
We begin to sink.

Without passion, we're reminded
To bring our seatbacks to their fully upright positions,
And to close our tray tables.
They will be in the aisle, soon, to pick up any remaining service items.
We will need them no longer, for we're on the glide slope,
Landing soon.

Last week my knee gave way and I fell.
Without passion, diminishment arrived suddenly, like an unwelcome guest,
Reminding me that I'm on another glide slope,
Landing soon.

Time passes as it did five minutes ago.
The view out the window hasn't changed much, yet.
The difference is in what happened just a moment ago;
Not the experience itself, but that unquiet, certain knowledge,
That now squats within: landing soon.

I wonder about my conveyance and what landing will be like.
The conveyance suggests nothing; neither I nor it planned this trip.
It works; I am aware of it, but not in any detail.
Fatally involved, I can only sit back and reflect about
Landing soon.

I don't recall taking off.
My seatmate shared her thoughts about the destination, but I
don't think she really knows.
The guy across the aisle scowls, doing Sudoku;
He seems urgent to finish, for he knows as we all do that we'll be
Landing soon.

I squirm in my seat, wishing it were over,
But glad it's not, just yet.
I am comfortable with the moment,
But the moment has no handle; there is nothing for me to grasp.
What difference anyway, when we're going to be
Landing soon.

Clouds lie beneath us;
Will landing be smooth or bumpy — who can know?
I feel like a man entering a darkened, unfamiliar room,
Fearing collisions or a fall; awkward.

All planes do return to earth, somehow.
We can only trust that they know what they're doing up there
And we won't crash.
They've dimmed the lights now, and I know it's time,
To shut my eyes, tighten the seat belt and hope for the best:
We'll be landing soon.

Questions For Discussion

1. What is this poem describing?
2. How do ruminations about your own demise go?
3. Is your heart troubled by you own impending death or that of a person close to you?

Waterfall

The promise of Easter sits brooding
Like fog on this waterfall.
Water rushes somewhere,
Into an abyss, as if on a mission.

Like thunder, it falls unbidden, unchecked,
Received, broken on unseen rock.
So you too rush somewhere within
Unbidden, unchecked and irresistible.

My broken life receives you,
Thirsts as only rock can;
Glistens with wet,
Hardness eroding.

In time it vanishes,
Water flows as always.
Overwhelmed, rock now soil bears mute witness,
To life stirring among its grains.

Questions For Discussion

1. The poem speaks of God's transcendence. Have you had an experience of such in your life? Explain in loving detail.
2. How would you characterize "thirst" for God?

I Met My Neighbor At His Place

I met my neighbor at his place,
To discover the reason he has a body,
And other things like that.

He has no idea, nor do I.

Whether there's a reason at all
Is likely immaterial;
The fact's indisputable:
There he is, unmodeled by words or equations.

Reason's too poor a medium to convey what's present.
Provenance and destiny are no match
For presence.

He prepares tea, as is his custom,
And begins to speak, summarizing the vast
Into a few words that make him look good.

I nod, as is the custom and paint
Without looking at the canvas.

The tea is too hot.
Like our conversation, it will cool shortly
And become quite easy to swallow.

Questions For Discussion

1. How does "God talk" strike you?
2. In your own words, compare direct experience and description. How would you characterize the difference, and how might it affect the way you actualize your faith?

Infant Baptism

Water…words…a name.

The nurse wipes off and leaves,
Aware of how this ends.
The door shuts with a pneumatic gasp,
Like the sound of someone's last breath.

We're alone now with your firstborn,
Who neither moves nor cries.

Sadness heavy as damnation
Squats in the room,
Like an unwelcome visitor who will not leave.

Quiet, we stroke a tiny cheek
That will never chew;
Never speak;
Neither smile nor laugh,
Or feel the heat of tears.

We gently touch cold, purpling lips
That will never kiss,
Pursed as if tasting the common bitterness
That comes unwelcome to us all.

Receding, he leaves as quickly
As a sudden change of mind.
I sigh and share tears, for I know,
Much more than a little life is over,
And much has just begun.

Questions For Discussion

1. How do you console someone who has suffered an unspeakable loss?
2. What words and sentiments "work" and which don't?
3. How can people find the presence of God in situations such as that which the poem describes?
4. What do you think "has just begun" in the words of the poem?

Learning To Center

Quietly sinking into depths of consent
Purely open to Presence and Action,
The chatter ceases to pretend
To be what I am.

What remains is nameless;
Blown by the winds of opinion,
Misgivings of memory,
Vagaries of emotion,
Yearnings inarticulate.

Beneath this layer,
Where Kool-Aid's unknown, and
Vance Packard has no purchase,
Lies the Greater Unconformity.

Quietly, nervous consent descends,
Without Virgil,
Past the campsite of Gilgamesh, with only
A nod to crazy Utnapishtim.

Deeper than death,
Deeper than life,
Into darkness blacker
Than darkness visible.

Suddenly there is nothing, and
Everything's clear.

Questions For Discussion

1. The poem describes an experience of Centering Prayer.[30]
2. The poem references a variety of people and themes. If you know what they are, consider how they fit. If not, try looking on the internet or Wikipedia.
3. What do the last two stanzas suggest about this form of prayer?

---

[30] https://www.contemplativeoutreach.org/sites/default/files/private/method_cp_eng-2016-06_0.pdf, June 9, 2019

Visiting Your Grave

The trees bend,
As if hearing unbearably bad news.
The wind, indifferent,
Rushes over gravesites,
Indifferent.

No different,
The cold winter sun
Broods behind clouds one
No different than another.

What difference does any of it make,
Rushing, bending, blowing?
You are dead,
And everything's different.

Questions For Discussion

1. What's different when a person dies?
2. Is "everything" really different? Why or why not?
3. What is the "sympathetic fallacy" and how does it play out in this poem?

The Pantheon

Welcome to the Pantheon,
Here you can choose your god.
Start in the Hall of Mirrors,
For most find their god in there.

When you weary of distortion,
Try another room, for the Pantheon is large.

Here is the Hall of Ritual,
You may find a god to your liking.
Choose your scriptures, icons, rites,
And other tools of control.

Here is the windowless Hall of Atheists;
One at a time please, for the room is small.

Over there is the Hall of Wealth,
Larger than all others, conspicuously magnificent;
You can measure your god in there,
Find ways to spend your righteousness,
And prove your worth,
If the others let you in.

Down the stairs to the left
Is the Hall of Vanity,
Where you will be allowed to write
Poems like this.

Hall after hall beckons,
Each with its own appeal,
Full of the emptiness
Of chosen gods.

When you start to cry,
Tug my hand and we'll go outside.
Stare at sky, feel warmth,
The bug on your skin, silent water.

There perhaps, you will intuit
What loves without being chosen.

Questions For Discussion

1. Who is your God and how did your discovery go?
2. What's wrong with a "chosen god?"

Psalm 139 From Another Point Of View

You seek, sensing presence.
Imagining absence.
My ways are clearly hidden.

Before questions are asked your responses are known;
You are penetrated through and through.

Where can we meet?
Why do you hide?
Climbing the heavens, you miss Me.
Lying in the grave, *all is lost!*

In silence deeper than death,
My right hand grips your being,
Like fingers in a glove.

You say, "let darkness hide me,
And the light around me be as night,"
But you grasp neither darkness nor light;
Time, so obvious, is a mystery to you.

I created your being,
Part of the warp and woof.
I offer you delight and wonder.

I knew you in secret,
Forged you in the furnace of stars.
My story requires your every day
To be exactly so.

To you, how mysterious My thoughts
Though you are one of them.
What you call "you" is not you at all,
Nor is my story Me.
Your search for Me is your search for you.
You will find what you never thought.

Questions for Discussion

1. Read Psalm 139. How does this poem reflect similar thoughts? Is anything different?
2. What does the last line mean?

Secrets

Secrets call darkness home.
Not the darkness of earth,
Not the darkness of oceans,
Not the darkness of sleep,
No place where things live and grow,
But someplace else.

Another darkness, the evil kind,
Clutches the living death of secrets
That find their home within;
Like the odor of open wounds
Infected, always untreatable,
And fatal.

Secrets squat in the dark pools of vanity,
The 'guilty thing' that will never be surprised,
In the unspoken haunts of Narcissus,
Within pain too severe to be forgotten,
Guilt never to be admitted.

Like cold vomit, the freedom secrets promise
Coat the cloth of which exteriors are made
Protesting innocence,
Where no such purity exists.

What will happen,
When Light penetrates this darkness?

Questions For Discussion

1. What is the poet's opinion of secrets? Why might that be?
2. Why do we keep secrets? Is there a time a place for them? Which secrets have neither good time or place?

The Anchor

We turned our rented boat into the channel slowly,
To the place we knew we'd find weakfish.

There were rocks here,
Deep enough to be invisible,
But solid enough to put a hole in our boat.
My job was to look for the rocks.

Helplessly, I scanned the water,
And hoped we wouldn't hit one.

My brother turned the motor off,
And we drifted to where the weakfish were.
"Drop the anchor," he said in a whisper,
(you don't raise your voice around fish),
And I secured the bitter end to a cleat.
"Slowly," he whispered.

I lowered the anchor over the side, line in hand,
Watching it slide slowly out of sight,
Into the murk below.

You can tell when an anchor hits bottom;
It always comes as a surprise.
There's a thud in the line and then slack.
You leave enough so that the angle isn't too steep,
Then you pull and set the thing.

The line goes taut and the boat swings
Bow to anchor where it went down.
If it's set right, you can look all around you,
And see you're not drifting.

It's like that with You, too.
I vaguely remember the anchor going over the side,
Many years ago now,
Disappearing in a wavy haze and passing out of sight.
I don't know if it ever hit bottom,
But the line's taut.

Question For Discussion

1. What other life experience of yours seems similar in significant ways to your apprehension of the divine?

On The Trail

The dog and I were walking
On the trail at the base of the hill,
Just sniffing around and thinking stuff,
As dogs and humans will.

Among the weeds, a glistening turd,
Captured his eye with its shine.
At moments like this, I'm exceedingly glad,
His habits are his, not mine.

With canine fervor he sniffs and circles,
Extracting the tale of the turd.
I watch, disgusted, patient with his habits,
Uttering not a word.

He finds it *delicious*!
I yank him away, he struggles to return;
From experience though, I've learned it's best,
To leave those turds on the trail.

Marveling at his revolting habits,
I notice with a certain unease,
Another creature's been pondering,
The turds it sniffs in the breeze.

Glistening memories of many times,
I'd just as soon forget,
Dot the trails of my life and stink like hell,
With the odor of regret.

With human fervor,
I sniff and circle,
Reliving the tales of those turds.

Though I know what's best, I find them delicious,
And try as I might, I fail;
It's simply beyond the strength I possess,
To leave those turds on the trail.

Perhaps when I'm older I'll leave them there,
As attractions wane and pale,
For there's peace of mind and lots less pain,
When turds are left on the trail.

Questions For Discussion

1. What's this poem really about?
2. What's so hard about letting go?

The Smartest Guy In The Room

As welcome as a toothache
Is the smartest guy in the room.

Never mistaken, always right,
(and, parenthetically, self-righteous, tedious, verbose and dull),
Pretense and derision is all that comes,
From the smartest guy in the room.

None are too humble,
To be spared disdain;
None too wise,
To merit acclaim.

No god but him,
His own lonely prophet;
Knows all about plugs,
But not the socket.

Lusting like an alpha male,
He soon defeats the flock,
Who feel his terror, knowing well,
There is no key to his lock.

The smartest guy in the entire room,
Knows this truth in his heart;
That airless, lifeless, empty gloom,
Where love never plays a part.

The terror he thinks he hides so well,
Is clear to those who'd call it hell,
Afraid of love, he has sealed his doom,
The smartest, the saddest, guy in the room.

Questions For Discussion

1. Have you ever been the smartest person in the room, in fact, or just in your own opinion? What was that experience like for you?
2. Does the experience bring you closer to God or farther away? Why might that be?
3. Describe you own experience of being, or being affected by, "the smartest guy in the room."

Parables

Jesus liked to explain to people how it goes in the kingdom of God using parables. Who am I not to follow *the way*? What follows are parables written for my lovely children at times when life wasn't going the way they thought it ought.

The Parable Of The Bowl

Once upon a time, there was an old wood-turner who liked to make beautiful things out of wood. Sometimes things would turn out well, and other times they wouldn't. That's not exactly true, though, as the parable will tell.

One day, the wood-turner decided to make a shallow bowl out of bloodwood — a lovely, hard red wood from wherever bloodwood comes from. He carefully worked with the wood and let it tell him what shape it needed to be. Slowly, the bowl took shape, and the wood-turner was very happy.

But the wood-turner didn't really understand something very important, and for a while took great pride in saying that the bowl was turning out just the way *he* wanted it to. Of course, that's simply not the way life unfolds.

One day, the wood-turner was working on the bottom of the bowl, trying to remove the screw holes that had held the bowl to the chuck. The screw holes were quite deep, and the wood-turner began to wonder when he'd be getting to the bottom of the deepest one. More and more material came off, until suddenly, the whole bottom of the bowl flew off the lathe!

In that moment, the wood-turner knew the piece was ruined. You can't put a bottom back on a bowl!

Sadly, the wood-turner removed the bowl from the lathe and admired its now lost beauty. It would have been a very beautiful bowl, he thought, had it turned out the way HE wanted it. Now it was just an expensive mistake, to be taken to the woodpile and burned.

On the way upstairs to the fireplace, the bowl winked at the wood-turner, the way bowls do sometimes, and the wood-turner stopped dead in his tracks. Of course, the bowl hadn't turned out the way *he* had wanted it. The bowl had turned out the way something much larger in life needed it to be and had come to be what it had really been destined to be all along.

With a humble laugh, the wood-turner realized his real mistake and carefully finished off the bowl so that its true inner beauty and real purpose shone forth. The beautiful bowl is now a beautiful puzzle-holder!

Hardly a mistake, wouldn't you agree?

Which leads us to the Parable of the Puzzle of course....

The Parable Of The Puzzle

Once upon a time, there was a little ball bearing that lived inside a giant and perplexing puzzle. It hadn't always been this way. As a small glob of steel, the little bearing had started out unformed, unrounded and without a purpose. Over time, it had been turned into a shiny, perfectly round, brilliant and precisely engineered ball bearing.

"I'm going to be in a jet engine," the bearing had said to its bin mates back then.

"Baloney!" yelled one of the others. "You're going to end up in a greasy 203-K inside someone's washing machine, just like the rest of us!"

All the other balls in the bin murmured in agreement, but the little ball bearing didn't pay any attention to them.

Then came the day when their bin was lifted off the shelf and taken to the assembly line. The little ball bearing looked in horror as all the other ball bearings were shoved in between the inner and outer rings of plain old 203-Ks, each destined, she was sure, for someone's washing machine.

Her turn came, and she was plucked up roughly by the assembler. She could see the inner and outer rings of the next 203-K in the assembler's other hand when suddenly, he stopped. Someone had come up to him and was speaking, but the little ball bearing couldn't make out what was being said.

The assembler flung the little ball bearing back into the bin, picked it up and walked off to an office somewhere deep in the factory. It was quiet there, but in a few moments, another voice came into the office to join the assembler.

"We need a really shiny one," the voice said.

"Just one?" the assembler asked.

"For now," the voice said. "Have you got a shiny one?"

The little ball bearing could see the assembler scanning the bin and did its best to look good and shiny.

"Here's one," the assembler said, picking up the little ball bearing. "Shinier than most, I'd say."

"Perfect!" said the voice.

The voice put the little ball bearing in her pocket and things got dark. The little ball bearing was alternately excited and afraid as she was being carried around. This was much better than being in a greasy 203-K. Or was it, she wondered — how could she possibly know for sure?

Eventually the little ball bearing felt someone searching for her in the pocket.

"I hope I haven't lost it," the voice said.

"I'm here! I'm here!" the little ball bearing screamed, but humans can't understand anything that's not human, and the voice gave up.

"I'll go back and get another," the voice said sadly, and the little ball bearing began to cry.

"I'm really here! Find me!" she wailed.

"Oh, wait," the voice said, feeling around in her pocket one more time. "Here it is."

The little ball bearing wiped its tears off on the way out of the voice's pocket.

"Wow, that's a nice one!" another voice said. "Perfect!"

The little ball bearing breathed a sigh of relief. Whatever it was going to 'be' part of the voices thought she was the perfect one for the job.

"Maybe I'm going to be in a jet engine…" the little ball bearing allowed herself to think.

"It goes in here," the new voice said.

With a plunk, the little ball bearing found itself inside a plastic sphere, surrounded by unintelligible blue, white and gray shapes on all sides.

"This doesn't look like a jet engine to me," the little ball bearing thought. "Where am I?"

Suddenly, her whole world turned topsy-turvy. One of the voices had picked up the plastic sphere and was moving it around. The ball bearing got very dizzy. Every now and then she would fall off one of the shapes and fall against the wall of the plastic sphere. What was the point of all this, she wondered?

"This is a great puzzle!" one of the voices exclaimed, "No one will ever be able to figure it out!"

"A puzzle? Not the same as a jet engine," the little ball bearing thought, "but what exactly was a puzzle?"

The little ball bearing decided to ask one of the unintelligible shapes that were close by. After all, they were all manufactured parts too, so they all had a common language.

"I'm perplexed. What's a puzzle?" the little ball bearing asked a squiggly blue shape nearby.

"I have no idea," the squiggly blue shape said. "I just know that we're all in this thing together."

The little ball bearing was dissatisfied with that response, so she moves on to a gray shape that looked like it was part of a trap.

"What's a puzzle, gray shape?" the little ball bearing asked.

"I don't know much," the gray shape admitted, "but I think I'm part of something people have to wrestle with lots of times before they get the hang of it."

"So, a puzzle's just one challenge after another?" the little ball bearing asked.

"Maybe," the gray shape said, "I really don't have the whole picture."

Just then, the new voice put the puzzle down and left the room with the other voice, chatting excitedly together. Once again, it became very quiet in the office. The little ball bearing rested at the bottom of the sphere, with all the other parts over her head.

"Can't solve a puzzle unless you pick it up," a gray lever announced to no one in particular.

"Has anyone ever solved this thing?" a blue ramp asked.

"Not that I know of," the gray lever replied, and many of the other parts agreed.

"Maybe solving it isn't the point," a white piece opined.

"Well, what good is it if it can't be solved?" the little ball bearing asked.

"Maybe we're here just to be enjoyed, and to enjoy being enjoyed," a blue stair-like thing suggested.

"But what are we supposed to *do*?" protested the little ball bearing. "At least in a jet engine there's a purpose to being there."

"There's a purpose here, too," the white piece observed. "Maybe it's more about *being* something good than *doing* something good."

"Then we're all pretty futile, aren't we?" the little bearing whined angrily.

"Hardly, little ball bearing," said a big white piece. "Can you imagine this puzzle without you in it? How would it even work? Good thing you're bright and shiny too, so the voices can see you!"

The little ball bearing took that in and began to think better of herself and all the pieces around her.

"I'm beginning to see now," the little ball bearing said. "This wouldn't be much of a puzzle if any of us were missing, not just me."

The big white piece laughed and said "Right — now you've got it!"

And all the other pieces joined in the joy of the moment.

The little ball bearing still wondered if what the other pieces had said was true. She realized in that moment that there were just some things in life that each and every little ball bearing has to see for herself. She decided she'd pay very close attention to the voices next time they came in.

She didn't have to wait long. The new voice came back, picked up the puzzle and began to turn it around and around. The little ball bearing glided just the way she was supposed to, smoothly and effortlessly, exactly the way she'd been engineered to perform. The other parts sturdily hung together for her, and she could see the voice's face radiating delight.

Yes, the little ball bearing happily thought to herself. Maybe the puzzle wasn't really ever going to be solved at all. Somehow in the lovely, generous living and working together of all the pieces, including herself and the voice, everyone was being and doing what really mattered in the moment. It was perfect!

Blurbularia

From time to time, I've been asked to write blurbs for parish bulletins, The Speakeasy (a book review website) and other such venues. Sometimes people bring up themes they've read in these things, so it seems fitting to share them with a larger audience.

Euphonium

My youngest daughter plays the euphonium. She told me two stories one day that I'd like to share with you. The first occurred when she was taking a lesson. Her instructor interrupted her in the middle of a session and told her, "Meredith — no one wants to hear you play your euphonium."

Her immediate reaction was shock and discouragement — she'd thought she had been performing perfectly. But then he continued, "What people want to hear is you telling them 'I love you' through your euphonium. There's no other reason to play, and no other reason to listen." Her next reaction was to think 'Wow!' and feel powerful surges both of challenge and privilege.

It's like that in our lives, too. We react differently to the nurse or doctor who treats us with care and compassion than we do to the one who treats us like an anonymous inconvenience, even if they perform perfectly. It is the same with teachers, landscapers, CEOs, moms, dads — everyone, even deacons. Does everything we do with other people allow God to say to them through us, "I love you?"

The second story is about a time when she was about to perform solo in front of a large number of very important people. One of her bandmates came up to her and asked her if she was nervous. She thought about it for a few moments and said, "No, I'm not nervous at all. I'm excited!"

What a difference a word makes! To be nervous is to wallow in self-conscious doubt and fear of failure. To be excited is to relish the opportunity in our path, intent on doing the very best we can right then, utterly unselfconscious. The physical emotion is the same, but how we frame it makes it either toxic or exhilarating; the choice is all ours.

Are we nervous or excited about our relationship with God? Do we wallow sometimes in self-conscious fear, dwelling on our sins, weaknesses and failures? Might we not choose to be excited instead by the recognition that Jesus has definitively liberated us from the very things that are at the root of our fears?

There's nothing more exhilarating in this life than to permit ourselves to give freedom to that growing awareness within us of wonder at the amazing God who became what we are so that we could become what God is. It leads pretty naturally into the praise, gratitude and respectful familiarity that are the hallmarks of the relationship between God and his friends. Cultivating love like this, we'll find that in no time at all, everything we do with other people allows God to say to them through us, "I love you!"

Questions For Discussion

1. Are you excited or nervous in your relationship with God? Why might it be that way?
2. What "instruments" do you play in your life? Who's in the audience?
3. How might you begin to say "I love you" through the many instruments that accompany you in your daily life?

Calling Jesus

A few weeks ago, I happened to be with a customer who's also a good friend. He's pretty well organized and there's a big board in his office that lists all the things he has to do. Without going into too much detail, I need to tell you that he has also led a complex life and is estranged from his Catholic faith at this point because of some of the turns that complexity has taken.

I was surprised then to see, right at the top of his list the reminder "Call Jesus." When I complimented him on getting his priorities straight, he burst out laughing. The "Jesus" on his list was a Mexican landscaper that he needed to call about something.

I laughed too, but when we both stopped laughing, we found ourselves still staring at each other and he remarked to me, "You don't ever stop being a deacon, do you?" I told him no; no more than I could stop being a dad, a husband or his friend. Taking advantage of the spirit of the moment, I said that I hoped he'd be able to get in touch with Jesus and that the conversation would go well. He knew what I meant. I noticed a distant look in his eyes as we turned towards our work for that day; he smiled and said wistfully, "Me too."

Where's "Call Jesus" on our list of priorities? Right at the top, I hope. Sometimes I have this image of Jesus waiting by a phone somewhere, hoping that it'll ring, and that it'll be a call from one of us. Sort of the way parents and grandparents wait for their offspring to call, just to say "hi" or share a story with us; ready to help out in case there's an emergency of some sort. There are some people we're happy to hear from anytime. It's the same when we call Jesus, too — we can call anytime.

Questions For Discussion

1. When was the last time you called Jesus?
2. Under what circumstances can it be that someone calling you is the same as someone calling Jesus?

How Does Your Garden Grow?

It's harvest time in these parts. I hope your gardens and orchards did well this year. As for us, we've had the best apple crop we've ever had — hundred and hundreds of gorgeous, large, juicy apples! There are so many that we've had plenty to give away to friends and neighbors. As I was out there up in a tree, picking the not-so-low-hanging fruit, it occurred to me that God was gently teaching me a lesson about life.

We planted our trees about twenty years ago, fertilized them, pruned them, and watched them grow. In time, they began to bear a little bit of fruit. Now there's enough to spread around well beyond the circle of our family. The miracle of an apple tree and the offer of its bounty is all God's doing. All we've ever done is take care of what has been given to us.

So it is with God's love. It's planted within us at birth, gets nourished by family, community and sacrament, and shows itself first a little bit, in the love we show those in our families and then, as we grow, far beyond the circle of our family. The miracle of love and all the good things that come of it is all God's doing. All we have to do is help it grow, and then give our love to other people as freely as God gave it to us.

At our place, we like to think that when we give away apples, or a pie or some applesauce, a little bit of God's other miracle, the miracle of love goes with it too.

Questions For Discussion

1. When you reflect upon your life so far, can you discern any seeds that God has planted through you?
2. How is your garden growing these days? What, if anything, might need cultivation?

Let Go

A few years ago, the company I had worked for almost seventeen years was bought by another company. I remember the day that was announced as if it were yesterday. Many of us had suspected that something like that was afoot, but of course nobody knew for sure. Everyone was concerned about what would happen next, when it would happen, and whether or not any of us would have a job. The rules were that if you were 55 with fifteen plus years of service, you'd be eligible for retirement and medical. If not, too bad. It was October and I was 54. I wouldn't be 55 until January. I had missed by two months.

As it turned out, the weekend after the announcement was the deacons' retreat weekend, and I found myself at Holy Family Monastery, mulling over my prospects. I remember praying "Okay, God, time for a sign." Shortly thereafter I was in the bookstore there, wondering how God might respond when there, at eye level, was a sign. It said "Let go…" I remarked to myself, "Cute, God… nice way to let me know what's going to happen next."

I moved along, but later on it occurred to me that if God sent a sign, the least a person could do would be to buy the thing, so I shuffled back to the bookstore and grabbed the sign. While paying for it, there was another sign by the cash register — same kind of frame and everything. It said "Trust…"

The signs were $8 a pop. I grumbled to God, "Hey thanks for the sign — but this is getting expensive, especially for someone who's about to be 'let go'." But when God gives a sign, you cut the whining and just do what's indicated. It seemed that God wanted me to let go and trust, so that's what I did.

On the Monday after the retreat, I went to work and there was a memo that said, "Oh, by the way, the sale isn't going to be complete until next February. The 55 and fifteen plus rule kicks in as of then." It turned out that hadn't missed by two months. I had made it by exactly one. All I really had to do was to "let go" and "trust."

There are plenty of good folks who have lost their jobs lately.

Turns out not everyone has a story like mine; life is very good, but it can also be very hard. If your job happens to have disappeared on you, let me suggest to you to let go and trust God — He's called the God of surprises for a good reason.

Questions For Discussion

1. What does "letting go" mean? What does it feel like in the moment?
2. Describe a time when you've trusted God. How does that recollection make you feel?

Father Damien

My wife and I have just returned from a trip to the Hawaiian Islands. Aside from taking in the peace and beauty of this amazing place and its lovely people, we also wanted to visit the leper colony on Molokai, made famous by the recently canonized Father Damien Veuster. It turns out that patients still live there, and you can only get in by invitation. Even then, it's a hair-raising mule ride down a sheer cliff.

The story of the leper colony is too long and distressing to relate here. Suffice it to say that it's a stunningly beautiful yet haunting place, with tales of hidden suffering calling out to you as you walk past unmarked graves or take in the rock offshore where patients were thrown off ships to swim to shore, if they could. Under no circumstances can you take pictures of the patients.

Father Damien was sent from Belgium to minister to the outcasts at Kalawao and Kalaupapa. At first, the patients rejected him, angry about their own rejection, viewing his compassion as mere condescension. On his part, he was revolted by the shocking disfigurement of the patients and the appalling smell, not sure at all that he wanted to stay.

In time, as he began to learn the Hawaiian language and the patients' stories, treated the wounds of those who would let him approach, and prayed for guidance, he began to see that it was not only lepers that he was serving, but Jesus. He went on to build cisterns for water, farms for food, and other such works. As I heard the guide relate Damien's story, I recalled the words of today's gospel:

"…I was hungry, and you gave me food, I was thirsty and you gave me drink, a stranger and you gave me welcome, naked and you gave me clothing, ill and in prison, and you cared for me…."

Father Damien was only supposed to stay for a few weeks, but ended up staying sixteen years. How could a Good Shepherd abandon his flock, anyway? Eventually he succumbed to the same disease as those to whom he ministered. He would have it no other way.

We're home now and the experience lingers. It's not unlike

the way it felt returning from Haiti, too. No one can see suffering like that and remain unmoved. To see Jesus in other people, care about their suffering; to share our own suffering and allow it to be healed in the sharing lies at the heart of the compassion to which God draws us. He would have it no other way.

Questions For Discussion

1. Have you ever been to a place where the earth has spoken out to you, or where you've felt an unexpected intense feeling? If so, describe what it was like. Could you sense the finger of God in it?
2. How have you shared another's suffering? Can you describe the experience in loving detail?

Peek-a-boo

I've never met a baby that doesn't enjoy playing "peek-a-boo," have you? They all seem so surprised and delighted to hide or be hidden and then re-discover their playmates. Maybe this simple game that we play when we're little can give us some insight into the Easter experience, too.

People who study these things speculate that "peek-a-boo" helps children learn and trust that people who disappear from sight will actually return. Playing "peek-a-boo" helps children practice seeing someone go away and coming back...over and over again, until they are confident that that's what will always happen.[31]

The delight that children experience in the game is also tied closely to the experience they have of some form of control over what happens. In some sense, they feel they can *make* their playmate reappear. Of course, as we grow up, we come to understand that the person who "disappeared" never really went away at all, nor was it us that made them reappear.

So it is with Easter. Every time we celebrate Easter, maybe even every time we celebrate mass, and maybe even every time we simply take time out to pray, we encounter the risen Jesus Christ and review the lesson that he who has disappeared from sight will actually return. Of course, as we grow in faith, we come to realize that Jesus never really went away at all, and it really isn't us who make him reappear.

Saint Paul tells us that Jesus gave us himself at the Last Supper. It's the way in which his presence and life is concretely realized and spread in our community. Think about it for a moment — if you have no body, you certainly aren't present, are you? And if your body has no blood in it, it's not alive, right?

To receive Jesus' body and blood is to receive his presence and his life — to become his presence and life for ourselves and for those around us. It's how the resurrected Jesus remains present and alive from one generation to the next. Those who see that in the Eucharist know that it's just as Saint Paul says, it's no longer us who live, but Jesus who lives within us.

---

31 http://pbskids.org/rogers/make_believe/peek.htm

It might take a fair amount of living before that becomes evident, but when it does, it's as if God suddenly looks at us from behind the veil of our limited understanding, greets us with a smile and a wink, and tells us "Peek-a-boo, I love you!"

Questions For Discussion

1. When has God played "peek-a-boo" with you?
2. Given that each of us is a unique expression of God's love, and that we're here principally to learn to love and be in loving relationship with ourselves, each other, God's creation and God's God-self, why do we have a body?

The Wish

My friend Father Tony sent an e-mail out last week about Mary Ann Bird, who had written a short story titled *The Whisper Test*. The story's about her childhood. "I grew up knowing I was different, and I hated it. I was born with a cleft palate, and when I started school, my classmates mercilessly made it clear to me how I looked to them: a little girl with a misshapen lip, crooked nose, lopsided teeth and garbled speech. Sometimes they would ask, 'What happened to your lip?' I'd tell them I'd fallen and cut it on a piece of glass. Somehow it seemed more acceptable to have suffered an accident than to have to admit having been born different. I was convinced that no one outside my family could love me.

There was, however, a teacher in the second grade that we all adored — Mrs. Leonard by name. She was short, round, happy — a sparkling lady. In our school system, we were required to have a hearing test every year. I was virtually deaf in one of my ears, but when I'd taken the test in past years, I'd discovered that if I didn't press my hand as tightly upon my good ear as I was instructed to do, I could pass the test.

The day came for the hearing test and Mrs. Leonard told us to line up. One by one we'd go to the door of the classroom and stand there to take the test. I knew from past years that as we stood against the door and covered one ear, the teacher sitting at her desk would whisper something and we would have to repeat it back ...things like, 'The sky is blue' or 'Do you have new shoes?'

Finally, it was my turn. I went up to the door waited there for those words. But God put into her mouth seven words which changed my life. Mrs. Leonard said, in her whisper, *'I wish you were my little girl.'*"

There are low times in most lives. Times when we don't feel particularly good about ourselves; times when perhaps we feel we're not worth very much and don't deserve anyone's love; times when we might feel we've done something or failed to do something and don't deserve to be loved.

We can turn into a very dark alley if we mistakenly decide that we *feel* unlovable because we *are* unlovable. Jesus clearly tells us that no matter what *we* may think or feel about ourselves, *God loves us* — completely, unconditionally, as-is, and forever.

And the "us" that God loves is the real "us," — the vast, complex, beautiful and maybe even terrifying "us" we glimpse from time to time when we peek inside, beyond the masks we make for ourselves, beyond the mask-maker and into the fathomless depths known only to those who know themselves to be what they really are: living, creative expressions of God's wisdom, love and compassion. It's in this spot that we hear God whisper to us, *'You are my beloved child, so much like me. See?'* Take a look. It'll change your life.

Questions For Discussion

1. How do we go about looking at ourselves?
2. There are at least three stories in which we play a part during life:

    The Great Story of All Creation
    The Story of Our Life
    The "...tale told by an idiot, full of sound and fury, signifying nothing."[32]
    In which story might we most likely find our true self?
    With which story are we most familiar?

---

[32] https://www.brainyquote.com/quotes/william_shakespeare_155103, June 10, 2019

Denial

A man and his wife were sitting in the living room watching a TV show about end-of-life issues. After a while, he turned and said to her, "Honey, I never want to live in a vegetative state, dependent on some machine and fluids from a bottle. If that ever happens, just go ahead and pull the plug."

His wife looked him in the eye and asked, "Are you absolutely sure?"

"Yep," he said, "that's what I want." So, she shrugged her shoulders, got up, unplugged the TV and threw out all of his beer (Thanks to Father Tony in Mobile, Alabama, for that).

The story points out a problem all of us guys have to face from time to time. Life is hard — sometimes it's downright brutal — sometimes it's even worse than that, and there's no assurance that it's going to get better, ever — not in the near term and not long term either. Life and our choices twist us into situations that are just plain hard for us to deal with. Times like these test our faith — like Job we wonder, where *is* God, anyway? Can't he *see*? Doesn't he *care*?

The answer is yes, God's around — closer to us than the nose on our face. Yes, he does see, and yes, he does care. It takes time to play out the hands we've been dealt and yes, both the stress we experience and whatever patience we can bring to bear in our situation define the nature of the outcome.

Many of us have lost our jobs and our businesses in economic downturns. Talk about life being hard — imagine watching the clock running out on your severance and benefits. And you're the dad, responsible for taking care of your family. Some have lost family and friends, others their health, some even more than that. Yep, life's hard.

How easy it would be to turn on the TV and crack open a beer — to deny that anything's awry and lose ourselves in a fog of fantasy, denial, and irresponsibility? How hard it is to accept what is happening to us, clear-eyed and non-judgmentally.

Questions For Discussion

1. Why is it so difficult sometimes to sense the presence of God when times are bad?

2. Avoidance and denial are the mind's defense against sudden, strong emotional situations, and are perfectly okay in the short term, provided you're not in life-threatening circumstances that require clarity of vision and acuity of thought. In the long term, they might not be very helpful at all. Left unattended, ungrieved losses and such like can be fatal to ourselves and others. What ways might you suggest for people to maintain vigilance in the face of denial and avoidance?

Fathers' Day — Happy Birthday!

I remember my son's birth as if it happened last week. My wife and I had gone to Lamaze classes and learned all the breathing techniques that were supposed to make labor a breeze. The process turned out to be more like a hurricane, but all of a sudden, there he was — my little baby boy, howling like a banshee.

They wiped him off a bit, wrapped him in a little blanket and handed him to me. I held him up close to my face and began to sing "Happy Birthday" to him. He immediately stopped crying and gave me a long, piercing stare. There's no way he could've known who or even what I was; there was nothing in his short life that he'd ever experienced that could've prepared him. But babies can hear what's going on outside their mom's womb, I'm told, and that's likely what happened. I think he recognized my voice and, in that moment, he stopped crying and knew for sure that he was safe.

It's like that with us and God, too. There's nothing in our material existence that can tell us what God's like, but we do hear God's voice — in the voices of our parents, teachers, and others who guide us, and in the wordless song of the creation in which we are immersed. Hopefully, these voices tell us that we are good, that we're loved, and it's that way because we are all made in the image of God, who *is* love.

On Fathers' Day, we want to encourage our dads to be windows into God's goodness. By 'dads' I mean biological dads, stepdads, and all good men who have stepped up to the noble and daunting challenge of fatherhood. Just being a dad who's present to his children is so very important.

Consider these facts from www.fathersforgood.org: half of all children with highly involved fathers in two-parent families reported getting mostly A's through twelfth grade, compared to 35.2 % of children of nonresident father families; children in father-absent homes are five times more likely to be poor, and more apt to spend time in prison. Dads *do* matter. It *is* up to you.

The transition from child to adult is a monumental turning point in everyone's life. Youngsters whose dads are there to guide them around that curve, and the men who helped them do it, will find themselves in a radically new relationship afterwards. What kind of respect can compare with the respect we have for someone who helped us become who we really are? What more can a dad ask than that his children grow up to be their own men and women, confident and unafraid, living life to the full, with the power of the love of God at the very core of everything they do? If our dads are good like that, what indeed must our heavenly Father be like?

Questions For Discussion

1. If you're a dad, how would you describe what being a good dad is?
2. If you're not a dad, what would you say about being a good dad?
3. In some sense, the principal role of a father is simply to give. What have dads got to give?
4. What has God got to give, and when does God give it?
5. What do dads demand back for all they've given (trick question, that one!)?

Gardening

Our garden has been growing for over a month now. It amazes me how fast weeds spring up out there. Every day I go out there with the hoe, hack the place up and then go in close to the stems by hand to get those nasty little horrors that are too close for the hoe to get.

It's tedious work, as many of you well know, but I happen to like it, because in the end we get to harvest beautiful flowers and tasty veggies. And there's nothing quite like taking something fresh from your garden either to brighten up the house or to eat. God makes the plants grow — my job is just to see that they grow into the best plants they can be.

Our lives are a bit like that, too. God made me, and it's just my job to grow into the best person I can be. It can be tedious work sometimes, keeping the weeds of evil out of the gardens of our souls. Some of them come out fairly easily with the hoe of prayer. For example, we can choose to acquire a good habit to replace one that's perhaps not so good, like putting a bible or a magazine like *Liguorian* or *Catholic Digest* where the beer or potato chips are. Yes, you can really put magazines in the refrigerator. Just keep them away from the wet and smelly stuff.

Sometimes you'll take out all three items and enjoy them together, maybe sometimes you'll decide you just need the reading material, and maybe other times it'll be just the chips and beer. No matter what, you'll have seen the magazine and have been reminded of the God who loves you, and that's the real point. Becoming a bit more mindful of God is a good first step in getting the hoeing done.

Close-in weeds are another story. Sometimes it's a good idea to get some help from someone whose eyesight is better or who perhaps has more patience than we do. It can help prevent ripping out the good plant along with the bad.

It's like that in ditching a bad habit, too. On our own, we can get discouraged or maybe not even see what really has to change. Sharing with someone we love our new mindfulness of God and our choice to drop a bad habit or two can be a pretty smart move. No need to do damage to what's really good about ourselves in the process of getting rid of those close-in weeds and becoming the best persons we can be.

Questions For Discussion

1. Describe some of the weeds in your garden, lovingly. What are you doing about them?
2. How do you handle those "close-in" weeds that involve other folks?

Mint

When we bought our house twenty-something years ago, I decided it would be fun to have an herb garden. I sent away for some herb plants and in a week or so the sage, thyme, chives, rosemary, and a few other wonderfully fragrant herbs arrived. So did the mint.

Now, if you've never grown mint and happen to plant some in your herb garden willy-nilly, you will find that in a few short years, your herb garden will have become your mint garden. You see, there's a right way and a wrong way to plant mint.

An invasive species of unparalleled determination, improperly planted mint will creep all over your garden and destroy everything else in it that's not mint. It will go into the lawn, behind the shrubs and, if you let it, into the house, past the dog's cage, up the stairs, and all over your bedroom too.

The trick with mint is to plant it in a pot, so that its rhizomes can't reach out and spread. Mint knows this trick, however, and even if you plant it in a pot, eternal vigilance is the price one must pay for a decent herb garden that happens to have mint in it. You simply have to get out there on a regular basis and snip off those nasty little runners that want to creep out of the pot and all over the place.

Last weekend I was excavating my herb/mint garden, with a mind to start over properly. I was thinking largely unlovely and unprintable thoughts about mint, when it occurred to me that God was teaching me yet another lesson about life. "Look Tim," God said, "Your sinful habits are like the mint, except they don't smell as good. Once you let something like that get a toehold, they'll take over your whole soul if you give them the chance. And just as you're finding out with the mint, it's hard work ripping them out."

"No kidding," I replied, stopping the tiller for the umpteenth time to clear out the mint roots form the tines. "Yes, Tim, and you'll also find that the price of a happy soul is constant vigilance." I was puzzled about this. "Does that mean I have to be a navel-gazer, constantly fearful and on the lookout for sinful habits?"

God laughed the way he does when we say stuff like that. "Not at all, Tim. What I mean is that you need to be constantly vigilant for my presence in your life. Trust me when I tell you that I know in detail what I have made and Tim, I love it all, including you and the mint."

"It's when you're not vigilant about my presence that the roots of sinful habits can get a toehold. If you're vigilant, we can nip them in the bud, just the way I know you're planning to do with the mint in your herb garden."

"Yep," I told God, "This time I'll get them all as soon as they show up." "Right," God said, though I sensed that if God had eyebrows they would've been raised just then. "Stay in touch," he said. I agreed, and that's where we left it.

Questions For Discussion

1. How would you describe "vigilance" in this context? Is it the same as anxiety?
2. What are the "invasive species" in society these days? In your life?

Gravitationally Challenged

A few weeks ago, I happened to mention casually to another member of the family that I was feeling gravitationally challenged. The aforementioned person seized upon this and decided to unearth Weight Watcher™ materials from long ago and make me do it. Being an agreeable sort who generally knows what's good for him, in many senses of that expression, I agreed that yes, I needed to do that.

For those who have never tried it, it's an excellent program that enforces awareness and discipline. Done with regularity, and along with appropriate exercise, eating habits improve and the weight comes tumbling off. The only thing I don't like about it is that I cannot eat whatever I want when I feel like it. But that's really the whole point, isn't it?

I was chatting with God about this the other day and he said "Tim, do you really think this little episode in your life is about weight?" I told him that I didn't think he'd be asking a question like that if that was all it was about. "Right!" God observed. "So — what do you imagine it's about then?" he asked. I told him it was probably about becoming aware of all the not-so-good things I did and acquiring the moral discipline to shape up. "Man," God said, "you *are* a slow learner."

Then he explained that the awareness he was looking for was awareness of him and his action both in my life and the lives that mine happened to be intersecting at the moment. The discipline he was looking for had nothing to do with how muscular my suppressive and repressive powers of self-discipline could get, but rather with a gentler discipline of mindfulness — a capability to sense his goodness welling up from inside. The discipline was about choosing more and more to prefer to be like him, and to do stuff to bring that goodness out into my little hunk of the world.

"Will I lose weight?" I asked. "Yep," said God. "You'll lose the weight that makes you feel as if you have to accomplish your salvation all by yourself; the weight that makes it feel as if there are all these rules weighing you down all the time; the weight of self-loathing when you mess up."

Since I generally know what's good for me, I told him I'd

give it a shot. "There's a catch," God mentioned. "What's that?" I asked. "You have to do whatever you want." "How is that a catch?" I asked. "It's like this," God said, "whatever you want will only be good for you if what you want is the same as the goodness for you and for everyone that I want. You have to accept my gift." "Gift?" I asked. "Yes," God said," the gift of deep knowledge of my ways, and the law of love." "How can I ever know what you know?" I asked God. "You can't," God said. "You have to let me live in you. I'll do the heavy lifting for us." I thought that was a pretty good deal, so I've signed up. Got any weight to lose? You might want to give it a shot, too.

Questions For Discussion

1. What's weighing you down these days?
2. What kind of diet would you consider embracing to deal with what's weighing you down?

Being A Deacon

Much of what's involved in being a deacon happens outside the parish. For example, a couple of times a week I take a break from work and visit folks in the hospital. It's the best job in the house, I think. All I have to do is show up and listen, perhaps talk a bit or pray if that's what folks want to do. I try to visit everyone in the wing to which I'm assigned, regardless of people's religious preferences or lack thereof.

Like most service, there's more received than given. I've found that everyone has a unique and fabulous tale to tell. One man wrote a book about Carl Yastrzemski (Red Sox fans know who this is and can also pronounce his name). Another survived the Holocaust. It seems that everything that can happen to a person in life and every emotion there can be lies there in wait, to be discovered, acknowledged, and cherished. Many times, it's not just the patient who wants to talk — it's the visitors too. It can be frightening to have a loved one in the hospital.

Almost without exception, people are grateful to have someone come in and break up the day. Sometimes the visits are brief and sometimes they go on for hours. Sometimes they are matter of fact and other times they are intense and personal. Sometimes I arrange for Father James to come for Reconciliation or the Sacrament of the Sick. All the time, I listen.

Occasionally, people will ask why I do this. I tell them that over time, it has become clear that I — along with the patient's family, friends, doctors, nurses, PCAs, co-workers, and everyone else who built the hospital and has ever had anything to do with how it runs — am a clear and visible expression of God's compassion towards his creatures, and God's involvement with our suffering.

I tell them that I was once in their shoes, and nobody visited. I tell them that there are two possible responses a person can have to indifference like that: withdrawal in angry bitterness or engagement with compassion. Knowing what it felt like, when the opportunity arose, I chose to engage and volunteer to help.

There's a deeper reason, too: God's reason. You see, it seems that service is redemptive. Twenty years ago, you wouldn't have found me even thinking about doing anything like this. God has drawn me to this service to show me something important about himself, myself, his creation, and how it all works together. There are new observations, awakenings, choices, and changes to make — some, I suspect, with eternal ramifications. Service is like that, and I stand in awe within the gift. Perhaps in your service, you do too.

Questions For Discussion

1. In what ways has God called you to serve?
2. Does service require ordination? What does ordination add to the mix? What does it restrict?

Grandparents

My lovely wife Chris and I became grandparents a few weeks ago. Everyone had told me how wonderful it was going to be, but having never experienced it myself, I had been skeptical. Then it happened and all those folks turned out to be right — it's wonderful! Little Henry is doing just fine, and his parents and grandparents are exhilarated too, in ways that are difficult to express fully.

As I held him in my arms at the hospital and sang him "Happy Birthday," I was reminded of the observation made by the Indian poet and Nobel Laureate Rabindrinath Tagore, who said that "Every newborn child is proof that God has not yet given up on mankind."

I stared at his perfect little fingers and toes and wondered what life had in store for him. The same thought had gone through my head when each of my own children had been born. Is there a good parent or grandparent who does not wish the choicest blessings of God for his or her offspring?

A few years ago, I'd found a poem by Dorothy Law Nolte entitled *Children Learn What They Live*.[33] Each line of the poem begins with "If a child lives with _____," and ends with "he will learn to be_____." It doesn't take much deep research to connect every part of the poem to something Jesus teaches us in scripture. Afterward, several folks wanted a copy of it, so I provided the link you see in the footnote.

The message seems as fresh and relevant now as it did back then. Take a look and see if you agree. Somewhere within are hints on how you and I can be the channel of God's choicest blessings to our children and grandchildren.

---

33 http://www.empowermentresources.com/info2/childrenlearn-long_version.html June 11, 2019

Questions For Discussion

1. After you've read Dr. Nolte's poem, try making up some lines yourself. For instance, how might a line that began "If a child lives with faith" end?
2. What prevents us from treating our children as well as we know we're capable?
3. How do you view children through the eyes of your faith as it is today?

Christmas Gifts

Looking for the perfect Christmas gift? Me too. I like to buy Christmas gifts. There's actually something prayerful about taking the time to find a gift that expresses something about the goodness, beauty or virtue of the person for whom I'm getting the gift.

I like to buy clothes for my wife that evoke some aspect of her fabulous inner loveliness; books for my daughters that resonate with their vast and deep spirits; complex things for my son that are in tune with his love of technological precision. I find that in the thinking about people, I actually find myself praying for them as I wander through the mall — thanking God for the wonder of their being; asking God to shower his blessings upon them as I ponder their goodness and unique gifts.

The perfect gift, no matter what it is, says "I know you, I care about you, and I love you." It occurs to me as I look for those perfect gifts, that any gift-giving I might be doing has its origin in the Giver of All Gifts, who gave us the Perfect Gift of His Son.

As I shop, I find myself thinking of our friends in Haiti. I'm struck by the contrast between the abundance surrounding me and the harshness of their struggle to live. It saddens me a bit, but I also rejoice to think that God has gifted us with the privilege of conveying his gifts of food, opportunity, and hope to them.

It occurs to me that the gifts we'd really like to give them can only be given by God. Nonetheless, we can pray for their safety, health, and well-being; we can pray that they may have a future full of peace and opportunity. Wouldn't that be the perfect Christmas gift?

Closer to home, I wonder about the people I meet in the hospital and what the perfect Christmas gift would look like for them. In my mind's eye I can easily imagine what these gifts might be, but I also recognize that these too can only be given by God. Although I know that, I believe that God reads hearts and in his infinite compassion will take my little prayer and shape it into the perfect gift these folks and their families really need.

I'd like to give the gift of one more day of life for the agitated man in the hospice wing who is afraid to die, that he may find peace. I'd like to give back to her family the mother of four who slammed into a tree not all that long ago and remains in a coma. Wouldn't a second chance for that seventeen-year-old who chose to drink and drive be the perfect present? Wouldn't the same thing for the 72-year-old who did exactly the same thing and killed his wife in the process come as a welcome surprise?

These gifts are beyond you and me. All we can give to their families and to them is the gift of praying for their peace and healing; that they may have a vivid sense that the love of God envelops us all, no matter what. In doing that, we become the perfect gifts through whom God gives the Perfect Gift of Himself to his lovely creatures who paradoxically both rejoice and suffer here on earth.

Questions For Discussion

1. What's the best gift you've ever received, and what made it so?

2. If you had to give your best friend a gift, what would it be, and why would you have chosen it?

3. If you were asked to give a gift to God, what would you choose to give? Why? Is it different than the gift you'd give your best friend? If so, gently explain why.

Compassion

One of the deep lessons people of compassion learn sooner or later is that we can only enter into another person's pain to the extent that we can enter into our own. Even in the short run, compassion can't be faked — suffering people can tell.

Entering into our own pain is not a journey undertaken lightly. I've watched some folks of perfectly good will walk away from the challenge. For them, there is simply too much unacknowledged suffering within, and they find it overwhelming to tackle it all at once. "Maybe after a few more years we'll be back," they say, "after we've done some of the work, we now know what we have to do."

Where does all this unacknowledged pain come from? Some of it stems from ungrieved losses. Death of loved ones, health problems, job losses, moving, disappointments and separations of one sort or another are all examples of losses that need to be acknowledged and situated properly in the collage that makes up the image we have of our life. I think you'll readily see that these losses are simply the natural conclusions of the good things that also come in our lives — the attachments to people, things and situations that give us security, love, joy and pleasure. Conclusions are perfectly natural, and to grieve them is as necessary and acceptable as it is to celebrate onsets.

In the long run, denial or repression doesn't really work as a way to deal with this kind of pain — ungrieved losses don't go away — they simply manifest themselves in other, perhaps destructive ways until we deal with them. Sometimes though, we just plain don't think about it, or refuse to give ourselves or other people permission to experience the painful part of a situation and develop ways to accept it. No one can do it for us, although compassionate people around us can help. People of faith know that prayer is essential.

There is a way to avoid pain, but it comes at a very high price. To avoid grief, love no one. Make no attachments and take no risks. In short — refuse to live. That'll do it, but I think you'll agree it's way too high a price to pay. From time to time, I see people at the hospital I fear may have made just such a deal. There's no family. No friends or acquaintances. Perhaps there's a defiant, crusty exterior, but almost always within there is a person who wants to be wanted: someone who wants to be loved. It breaks my heart to be with them in pain like that.

There's a poem by the thirteenth century German mystic Meister Eckhart that can help us understand what this feels like, and what's at stake. The poem is called *The Hope of Loving* and it goes like this:

> What keeps us alive, what allows us to endure?
>
> I think it is the hope of loving, or being loved.
>
> I heard a fable once about the sun going on a journey
> to find its source, and how the moon wept without her lover's
> warm gaze.
>
> We weep when light does not reach our hearts.
>
> We wither like the fields if someone close does not rain their kindness upon us.[34]

Questions For Discussion

1. Have you ever entered into your own pain? What was that experience like for you?
2. Have you ever entered into the pain of another? What was that experience like for you?
3. How might we best learn compassion?

---

[34] https://www.thehouseofyoga.com/magazine/"-hope-loving"-—meister-eckhart — in the public domain

Mistaken Identities

When I was in Haiti back in 1999, a little boy mistook me for Jesus Christ. I reassured him about his misidentification and we moved on. Mistaken identities can cause problems, especially when the identity about which we're mistaken is our own.

Counselors and psychologists are familiar with the masks (personas) that we build as we go through life. A persona is the face we present to the world; how we wish to be known. In some sense it's a selective distillation of all of our experiences, attributes and capabilities, as well as other people's opinions, grades, reviews and such like, packaged to enable us to reach our conscious and subconscious goals.

A persona is necessary for daily life, but it isn't who we really are — at least not entirely. We can get into considerable trouble if we believe that all we are is what we and others have made ourselves out to be. We may have created our persona, but we did not create our being. Only God does that.

Much of what we are is utterly hidden from us until someone points it out. It's always worth taking the trouble to broaden and deepen our view, because the exercise is essentially redemptive. It may be surprising or even frightening, but it always takes us closer to the view of ourselves that God has.

What might God's view look like? Psalm 139 tells us:
"O Lord, you have probed me, you know me;
you know when I sit and stand;
you understand my thoughts from afar.
My travels and my rest you mark;
with all my ways you are familiar.
Even before a word is on my tongue, Lord, you know it all.
Behind and before you encircle me and rest your hand upon me.
Such knowledge is beyond me, far too lofty for me to reach.
Where can I hide from your spirit?
From your presence, where can I flee?
If I ascend to the heavens, you are there;
if I lie down in Sheol [the grave], you are there too.

If I fly with the wings of dawn and alight beyond the sea,
even there your hand will guide me,
your right hand hold me fast.
If I say, 'Surely darkness shall hide me, and night shall be my light'
darkness is not dark for you, and night shines as the day....
You formed my inmost being; you knit me in my mother's womb.
I praise you, so wonderfully you made me; wonderful are your works!
My very self you knew; my bones were not hidden from you,
When I was being made in secret, fashioned as in the depths of the earth.
Your eyes foresaw my actions; in your book all are written down;
my days were shaped before one came to be...."[35]

It sounds like God has a pretty good handle on who we are. Perhaps we might choose to ask God to take us by the hand and begin to show us who we really are, not as we see ourselves, but as God sees us. God loves us and wants to bridge the gulf between us and him. Who knows, after we see ourselves the way God sees us, we might even want to do the same thing!

Questions For Discussion

1. Who do you think you are?
2. Who do you think others think you are?
3. What do you think God makes of you?

---

[35] http://usccb.org/bible/psalms/139, June 11, 2019

Silence

There's a story about three hermits who move into a cave together. For the first ten years they don't speak to one another. Then one day a chicken walks past the mouth of the cave. Ten years later the first hermit says, "I wonder why that chicken came along?" Ten years after that the second hermit says, "It wasn't a chicken, it was a duck." Another ten years go by, and the third hermit silently starts packing his bags. As he gets up to leave, the other two look at him with raised eyebrows. He turns to them and says, "Look, if all you two are going to do is argue, I'm leaving."

How are you with silence? As a chaplain in the hospital, I'm learning a lot about silence. It turns out there are different kinds of silence. For instance, there's the silence of a room in which people are sleeping. There's something about them that reminds me of the peaceful beauty of sleeping children. I never wake them — you probably wouldn't either. Instead, I quietly leave a card for them and vanish without a sound. Theirs is a silence of peaceful healing and mine is of one of simple respect.

There's a different kind of silence that emerges when, after introducing ourselves and getting past the routine pleasantries, patients begin to talk about what's on their mind. Before they go deeper, they study me quietly for a moment. I'm not sure whether they want to see if they can trust me or if they're tacitly asking for permission to continue. When I'm alert enough to pick up on what's happening, I gently touch their arm, look at them and say, "Tell me about that." It's an invitation to them to speak and to me to remain silent.

It's a vocal silence though, much like prayer. The wordless communication isn't from me — it's from God. Of that, I am certain. In its own way, that silence says to the patient: "You matter. I am not indifferent to your suffering, and I love you. You can say anything, and I will remain calm; I will not judge you."

Hearts are poured out into that silence. When we're not interrupted by the normal events that occur in a hospital, the conversation ebbs and flows like the tide coming in and going out. Frequently there are tears. Occasionally they are mine. Sometimes it can happen that I will have said nothing at all, yet everything that needed to be said has been said. It's an instance of the silence of the presence of God.

There are happy kinds of silence, too. When our children were little, we used to take time out every now and then before or after dinner and go around the table so that everyone could say something good about everyone else around the table. The rule was that everyone had to speak, and everyone else had to be silent while anyone else was talking. In this kind of silence, we were free to express and to drink in our family's love for one another.

There are other silences which aren't life-giving at all. The silences of moodiness, resentment, disdain, contempt and anger bespeak the need for power and control, and of course, the fear that underlies such needs. Silences like these are forms of domestic violence. They pull us away from each other and from God, into the self-destructive vortex of sin and narcissism.

Questions For Discussion

1. How are you with silence?
2. What has your experience of silence been?
3. If you wish to enter into silence, where might you situate yourself?

Recognizing Yourself

My daughter Kate and I like to trade stories. One day she was telling me about a conversation she'd had with a Maryknoll missionary, Father Jim. He had spent the last several years in Africa and was delighted by the cheerful innocence of the people he'd met in the remote villages he visited.

At one village far away from 'civilization,' he took out his digital camera and showed a group of young children how it worked. They squealed with joy as they pointed each other out in the pictures. But they were puzzled too, because each of them saw someone in the pictures they didn't recognize. Father Jim was puzzled too, because the village was small and remote enough so that there couldn't possibly have been any strangers among them. Then it struck him. There were no mirrors in the village — never had been. The people the children didn't recognize were themselves.

For better or for worse, most of us probably think we have a good idea of what we look like; mirrors are no mystery to us. But do we have a mirror in which we can see ourselves as others see us? For some of us, that mirror might be a loved and trusted family member with whom deep stuff can be safely shared from time to time. For others it's a good friend or reliable confidant outside the family.

For your mirror to reflect properly, he or she has to be trustworthy, fearlessly honest, calm and non-judgmental. In their own safe and gentle ways, our mirrors need to reflect us, as they see us, without distortion. Folks who are good mirrors will sense the right times to help us see our shadow side — those dimensions of ourselves of which we cannot be consciously aware on our own and which we might not even like — without hurting us.

It may seem risky to have mirrors like that in our lives, or to be one ourselves for other people, but without a mirror we're like the little kids in Africa were. We need to know what we look like- so we can come to accept and love ourselves. Without that knowledge, our capability to love one another is in peril, too, since we have to love ourselves before we can love anyone else.

A note of caution is in order here: avoid the temptation to be your own mirror, since we all tend to reflect distorted images to ourselves, like those crazy mirrors at the circus that make you look fat or stretch your neck like a giraffe's. Think about it — would you use a funhouse mirror like that to shave or put your makeup on?

One last thing about mirrors — in the very best of them, when you look, you'll actually see Jesus. Just for fun, take a glimpse in your own mirror and ask — does the image staring back at me look more like Jesus or more like someone else?

Questions For Discussion

1. How have you been a mirror to another person? What was that experience like?
2. When have others been mirrors to you? How do you see God operating in that?

Confirmation Interviews

A week or so ago, I had the privilege of interviewing a number of confirmation candidates. I was impressed by the maturity and poise of the young men and women, and I'm confident they will all do well as they continue to grow.

One of the questions I asked concerned how and when they prayed. In most cases, the young people said they found time for prayer at the close of day, when they were about to turn in for the night. It was a time when no other obligations could intervene, things were peaceful, and they could be alone with God. A few said they prayed at various other times during the day, whenever circumstances inclined them to become prayerful.

One of the young people reflected the question back to me and asked when I prayed. I told them that as a deacon I was obliged to pray the Liturgy of the Hours in the morning and at evening. Aside from that time of formal prayer, my day was alive with all sorts of perhaps less formal prayer.

I told them that my first conscious thought in the morning was a prayer of thanks for the privilege of being alive, safe, dry, well-fed, and happily next to my lovely wife, Chris. Then, if there was something difficult lying ahead in my day, I might pray about that, too. Just before getting up, there's a moment of self-offering that generally goes something like this:

"Dear Pop, I offer myself as you know that I am to you as you know that you are. Let me be a loving instrument of your peace and joy, kindness and goodness, so that when people see me, they see you; when they hear me, they hear you; and when they're touched by me they're touched by you. May Tim diminish, and you increase. I'm yours. Amen."

During the day I find that informal prayer has something of a life of its own. It's full of gratitude and praise, wonder, and joy. Prayer does for my life what spices do for food. Sure, you don't need spices, but man, do they make a difference in the way things taste!

I've told you about some of the prayers I've said in the hospital, too. There's an awesome overshadowing or overpowering feeling when God takes over. The best kind of prayer just then is an attentive, wordless presence; a sense of simply being ready, letting God take the initiative.

I'd read an article recently in which people who studied prayer across the boundaries of different religions reported that they'd found four common themes among people who pray, that could be summarized lightheartedly as follows:

Thanks. Wow! Oops. Gimme.

Gratitude, praise, repentance, and supplication. These four simple themes reflect what people express in their conversations with their creator. They sure sound familiar to me. Think about your own prayer life. Are these themes familiar to you, too? What does each theme say about you and what's going on in your life right now? Where does your God's response take you as you live out your day? Can you taste the spice?

Questions For Discussion

1. How do you pray? What works well for you and what doesn't?
2. How does prayer help us be the expressions of God's love we were created to be?

Situational Awareness

One of the things that's emphasized when you're learning to fly is "situational awareness (SA)." What SA means is that nothing escapes your attention as you check out yourself, your equipment, the weather, and the myriad other details that you need to grasp to create your flight plan, fly someplace, and return safely.

Successful (i.e., "living") pilots perceive, understand, and react effectively to every variable that can affect any aspect of flight. Nothing's ever overlooked; sage pilots know that Mother Nature sides with the hidden flaw. Ultimately, a pilot's SA skills determine in large measure whether he or she will return to earth in the same condition as when he or she left it.

In a reflective moment, it seemed to me that much of our ability to get by in life is like that, too. Just about everything requires us to be alert, understand what's going on, stay two steps ahead of the situation, and respond appropriately at all times. This explains sleep, I think. High SA is exhausting — who can keep it up 24x7?

The list of SA's enemies includes distraction, presumption, rushing through things, pride, and perhaps less obvious things too, like headaches. Anything that diminishes SA — our ability to perceive, understand, and respond appropriately — before, during or even after a flight can be fatal. Same goes in life writ large; relationships can crash and burn too if we lose sight of what's happening, fail to understand, or respond inappropriately.

Perhaps it's the same spiritually. Just as an airplane is subject to our choices as pilots, so our souls are subject to our moral decisions as humans. It seems to me that spiritual SA is even more important than day-to-day SA. If you're distracted at some point during a ballgame, you may miss the double play, but if you're continually missing the signals, you just may lose the game.

The enemies of spiritual SA are the same; distractions over career, money, and other peoples' opinions; presumption about what merits our attention and what doesn't; rushing through life so fast we miss its meaning. The less obvious obstacles are there too — bad health and an un-accepting disposition, resentments, petty selfishness — all these can a take person's SA clean down to zero.

Jesus taught us that he is "the way, the life, and the truth." To get what this really means, you need to know that the Greek word for "truth" is αλήθεια (alethia) — literally "not being asleep/unaware/dead". The Jesus that we invite into our hearts and share with one another is he who is fully alive, fully, and simultaneously aware of the human and the divine condition and at least two steps ahead of every situation we'll ever find ourselves in. Want your soul to fly? Let Jesus show you what SA really means!

Questions For Discussion

1. How do you maintain spiritual "situational awareness?"
2. What, in your experience, have been good ways to overcome distractions?

Excess

How's your garden coming along? Mine's doing fine — lots of jalapeño peppers, tomatoes, blueberries, and raspberries, potatoes, eggplant, and of course, the zucchini. Lots of zucchini. More than enough zucchini. Enough to feed *all* those little kids in India.

One evening last week, while I was picking the 4,297th zucchini from the squash patch, God dropped in.

"How's the garden, Tim?" God asked.

"It's coming along pretty well, God," I said, "except that I have lots more zucchini than I need."

"What are you going to do with the excess?" God asked.

"I'll probably give it away," I replied. "Would you like some?"

"It's already mine," God reminded me with a smile. "I'm sure you're planning to give it away to people who'll enjoy it."

"I will," I agreed, "I like to give good stuff away to my friends."

"How about the rest of your excess?" God asked me.

"There's not an excess of anything else, God," I said.

"I don't mean vegetables, Tim" God said. Somehow, I already knew that. "You want money?" I asked.

God laughed. "Guess again!"

"Prayer time?"

"Nope," God said, "remember, we're talking about your excesses here, Tim."

"Oh," I said, chastened. "What do you mean, then, God?"

"I've showered you and your family with an abundance of blessings, Tim," God said, "have I not?"

"You sure have, God," I said, "you've been very kind."

"Maybe even excessively kind?" God asked with a raised eyebrow.

"Well, yes," I said, "You've been kind to us beyond our dreams."

"Then why don't you give some of that excess kindness away along with your excess zucchini?" God suggested.

"Hmm, that might be fun," I said, warming up to the idea.

"Can you think of anything else which I've showered upon you in excess?" God wondered aloud.

"Sure, God," I said. "Just about everything! You've been so patient with me, and generous and compassionate, and…"

"Think you can give some of that excess away with your zucchini too, Tim?" God asked.

"I get it now, God," I said. "You know, I wasn't really through, either. You've been excessively forgiving, gentle and loving, too. The list goes on and on."

"Just like the zucchini, Tim?"

"Yes, exactly like the zucchini," I laughed. "There's *so* much!"

"Then give it away, Tim," God said. "you said you like to give good stuff away to your friends. I do too."

We stood there for a moment, looking at each other with affection, and I smiled as I thought of all the people who'd be getting not only a zucchini, but now so much more.

Questions For Discussion

1. What "excesses" have you experienced in your life, and how have you handled them?
2. What prevents us from perceiving excess?

Amnesia

A few days ago, at the hospital, I received a page to visit a man who had asked for spiritual support. I went up to his room and found a friendly, robust, physically fit man who didn't seem to be in any great distress. His wife was there too — very friendly too, yet eager to let us have some time to talk alone.

He told me that he had suffered an episode of transient global amnesia (TGA). That's a condition in which you simply have no memory of what has recently happened to you. It's not life-threatening and it's unlikely to reoccur, but it's frightening when it happens because although you remember who you are, a portion of your life is lost to you forever.

In his case, he'd found himself in a town nearby with no idea why he was there or how he'd driven there. It had shaken him up badly. "I've never been out of control before," he said. "I could've killed myself or other people and never even known what I was doing."

He turned out to be a well-educated person, with an impressive career in the military and later in corporate life. As I listened, the image began to form of a man whose identity and self-worth had been closely tied to his jobs and his performance in them.

It seems that he had retired not long before his TGA episode. I asked about that, and his brow furrowed. "I feel lost now," he said plaintively. "I'm not sure who I am any more or what I'm supposed to do." I told him that from a spiritual perspective perhaps his TGA episode was a gift from God — a touchstone, if you will.

Maybe now that he was retired, and there were no more corporate or military masks to wear, his spirit had encountered something within that frightened it. Perhaps something vulnerable had suddenly become exposed, something that was childlike and needy, something that wanted to love and be loved, that might've always been there, but had been ignored.

On the other hand, perhaps his spirit was telling him through the TGA that there was something about himself he wished he could suppress or forget. Only he could know for sure what it meant. I encouraged him to explore with God through those he loved and who loved him what the gift might mean.

I listened some more and was reminded of an observation a co-worker had shared with me decades ago. In a moment of blinding, bittersweet honesty, he had acknowledged his material success and in the same breath said he'd become "everything I *never* wanted to be." I wondered whether the patient in front of me would've described himself that way. Perhaps he might've even ruefully agreed with Thoreau that "most men lead lives of quiet desperation and go to their graves with the song still in them."

A chaplain's job is not to help people feel miserable about themselves, but simply to listen and perhaps say or pray a thing or two that might help a person explore themselves a bit more deeply and uncover the beauty and power with which he or she has been graced by God. So, I kept Thoreau and my co-worker to myself, but I do wish to share them with you. If you choose to think about them, consider doing so in the spirit of Mark 8:35-36: "For whoever wishes to save his life will lose it, but whoever loses his life for my sake and that of the gospel will save it. What profit is there for one to gain the whole world and forfeit his life?"

Questions For Discussion

1. In what ways might you have become everything you never wanted to be?
2. What songs remain to be sung in your life? What's preventing you from singing?

Fear

I was walking around the block the other day, admiring the loveliness of autumn, when God showed up and joined me. I said hello and we struck up a conversation.

"Does autumn remind you of anything, Tim?" God asked.

"Lots of things, God," I said. "What would you like me to see?"

"I'd like you to see that you're in the autumn of your life, Tim," God said. For some reason that sent a chill up my spine.

"Why are you afraid, Tim?" God asked.

"I'm not afraid," I replied quickly.

God wasn't buying that and just gave me one of those looks.

"Well, okay," I said, "I'm a *little* afraid. Sometimes I feel as if I haven't accomplished much in life, and that time's running out."

"And you figure I'll be waiting for you with your report card in one hand and a baseball bat in the other when you show up at the pearly gates?" God inquired.

"If I were you, I would be," I said.

"Good thing you're not me, wouldn't you say?" God observed.

I agreed, and we walked along quietly together for a while.

"Where does that fear come from, Tim?" God asked.

"Well," I told God, "When I see all the kids go back to school, I remember my own youth and how everything we did was graded. Later, it was performance reviews at work. It was always about other peoples' expectations, results, and judgment. I hated it when it was phony, and I feared it when there were real consequences."

God was quiet for a bit as we walked along. "Maybe it's not like that with me at all," God said. "Maybe what's really important is what you've become, rather than what you've done."

I was puzzled and asked God to explain a little more.

Always agreeable, God said "Sure. Have I ever shown you the book I'm writing?" I innocently said "no" and in that moment sensed a suppressed laugh. Then God handed me a small sliver of paper. "This is from a part closer to the end than the beginning," God said. "Read it aloud."

It wasn't even a full sentence. It just said, "...everything he could to ease the suffering of his beloved, and tasted suffering himself. They gazed deeply into each other's eyes with love and realized that without consciously knowing it they had become one."

I handed the slip of paper back to God and as I did so, God said "Tell me what the book is about, Tim."

"From one slip of paper?" I exclaimed. "I can't do that!"

"Good observation," God said. "Can you tell me what kind of story it might be though?"

"Sounds like a love story of some kind," I guessed.

"Right," God said, "those are the only kind I write. Would you like to be one of the characters in it?"

"I think so," I replied.

"Good thing," God said, "Because you already are. This is your story, Tim."

I stopped in my tracks, shocked. Then I asked God, "Umm... just how close to the end of the story was that little passage?"

"That would be telling, Tim," God said with a smile. "Will you let me create the character in you that I need in my story?" I was too awestruck to respond so God just said, "I'll take that as 'yes'." I felt God's arm around my shoulders, and we finished our walk together in happy silence.

Questions For Discussion

1. Describe a fearful moment in your life. What was the source of the fear? Can you touch your fear the way you can touch your nose? What does that say about the reality of fear?

2. Can you write a phrase that describes the love story of your life?

Teaching

I love to teach. There are several reasons for that. First, when you have to explain something, you have to come to know it well yourself. Doing the work to get a good grasp on something's inner logic is fun. It's also a thrill to see people make the connections that turn what you're teaching into something that's their own. The third reason's the most important to me, though. You see, I've always loved my students and wanted them to have a full life. To love, to teach and to learn is to enter deeply into the meaning of life, it seems to me. Let me tell you about teaching statistics, and you can see if you agree.

At the beginning of each semester, I explained that everyone was starting off with an 'A'. If they did what was required, they'd keep that 'A' and if they didn't — well, it was very simply theirs to lose. It was their choice. Some believed me. Some didn't. Like God's promise to us of love and an eternal life of joy, it was true whether they believed it or not. I encouraged them all to stop by, e-mail or call if they got stuck on any of the material. Some did. Most didn't. I wondered whether my own relationship with God and my prayer life in times of difficulty were like that, too. I can't speak for anyone else, but sadly I think at various times in my life it was.

Each student had to do a project in which they were to use any data that interested them and apply what they learned in the course. It didn't matter to me whether the analysis was fancy or simple. All I wanted to see was that they'd learned something about statistics.

At some level our life's a project about learning to love and to be loved. A life doesn't have to be fancy, long or short. I told my students that they could send me drafts of their project as they went along, and I'd help them and challenge them with different ways to look at their chosen data. A few students took me up on this. Most didn't. I was amazed that so few took me up on the offer. Maybe God's amazed that some of us don't go to him for help either.

On the take-home midterm and final, I gave them 250 questions. They could answer all 250, I told them, but I stopped counting after I'd found 100 correct ones. With 2 ½ times as many questions as they needed to keep their 'A,' it was beyond fair. But although some students answered more than 100 questions, most didn't. They just did the minimum. I thought about all the times in my life that I'd done just the minimum, too.

One day I was chatting about this with my friend Joe, who also teaches statistics. He shook his head and wondered aloud: "How much easier can we make it, Tim? Don't they see they're only hurting themselves?" What is it about us that prevents us at times from taking God up on his offer of love and acting in our own best interests? We didn't come up with an answer. Maybe you can.

Questions For Discussion

1. If God asked, how might you suggest God make things easier in life? What's behind your suggested improvements?
2. What keeps us from approaching God?

A Very Special Gift

So, what are you going to give God for Christmas this year, hmm? It's actually pretty easy to pick something out — all that's ever on God's list is love. That's all God wants, it seems — not only to get but to give. To ponder God's gifts is to see that everyone and everything is an expression of God's love, including us. Yes, we really are God's gifts to mankind, each and every one of us.

Let me tell you about some very special gifts, though. A while ago I was the on-call chaplain again at the hospital. Sometimes people ask to see a chaplain for a specific purpose, and this particular evening there was a request from a man in the palliative care unit for Communion and a visit.

"Palliative care" is the care patients receive when there's nothing more that can be done for them, medically. Patients are aware that death is coming perhaps sooner rather than later. Care given at this point is termed "comfort measures only" (CMO). It's good care, rendered as deftly and compassionately as normal medical care. It's just that everyone recognizes it's the end of the line.

I brought Communion to the man and sat quietly nearby as he prayed silently. Then he looked up and began to talk. He had much to say, and we spent almost an hour together. At one point he hesitated for a moment.

"I want to tell you something," he said, "but I don't want you to think I'm crazy."

I told him he could tell me anything and invited him to proceed. "Last night I sat in the lap of Jesus," he said in even tones, looking at me intently.

I calmly asked him to tell me what that was like for him.

"It was wonderful beyond description," he said. "I can't find the words to tell you how wonderful it was. It exceeded every expectation I'd ever had about what meeting Jesus would be like. I didn't want to come back."

We sat together quietly for a bit and then he continued. "I don't know if it was just a trick of my imagination or some chemical thing, but it was good. Do you think I'm crazy?"

I told him that I thought no such thing and asked if I could share a similar story about my mom. He agreed eagerly and I told of sitting alone with her one evening, quietly holding her hand as she neared the end of her life. All of a sudden, she opened her eyes and asked, "Timothy, who are all those people over there and why are they going up the stairs?" I replied that I thought they were all just going home. Her expression seemed to say "Oh, of course." Satisfied, she closed her eyes again, peacefully.

The patient with whom I was speaking listened with great interest and then said excitedly to me, "So you know about the stairs!" I nodded, and he asked, "What do you make of it?" I told him that the experience my mom had was quite common, and frankly, more the rule than the exception. At the end of life, it seems, we get what we need to be able to move on. It's one of our lovely God's most gentle and compassionate gifts to us.

Then I told him that Celtic Christianity speaks of "thin places," where the space between heaven and earth seems almost to vanish. My mom had been in such a place, and so had he. They're gifts to us from a loving God, I told him. You can always tell, for you see, God's gifts are not the kind that are wrapped — they're the kind that are lived, and they're all about love.

Questions For Discussion

1. Have you experienced a "thin place" in your life? What was it like?
2. What might have been the purpose of your gift?

New Year's Resolutions

How are you doing with your New Year's resolutions? If you're like me, perhaps you decided not to make them this year. After all, it can be quite dispiriting to resolve to do something and then fall on your sword before the ink dries on the paper.

Convinced of the superior logic of this approach, you can imagine how surprised I was when God showed up last week and asked me how I was doing with my New Year's resolutions.

"I don't make them anymore, God," I replied.

"Really?" God asked. "You mean you have no goals?"

"Oh, I have goals, God, but not resolutions," I explained, forgetting for the moment how pointless it is trying to convince God that my ways are better than his.

"What's the difference?" God inquired.

"Well," I told him, "A goal is something I plan to accomplish, and a resolution is something I'm just going to try to do."

"Give me an example," God asked.

"Losing weight," I said. "It seems I can resolve to lose as much as I want, and maybe even do it, but it keeps on coming back."

"All by itself?" God asked.

"Pretty much," I said. "You know how it is."

"Oh, I know how it is," God said with a grin. "Tell me — is it important to you to lose that weight?"

"Sure, God," I said. "Why else would I make a resolution about it?"

"Is it something you really want to do or just something you just think you ought to do?" God inquired.

"You want the truth?" I asked.

"Always," God replied.

"I do want to lose a few pounds, but food tastes *so* good!" I said.

"And you just can't resist it?"

"Something like that."

"Maybe you mean you don't want to resist it."

"Maybe you're right," I admitted.

We got quiet for a few moments, and then I said, "This conversation isn't really about weight, is it, God?"

"Maybe it is, maybe it isn't." God said. "What do you think it might be if it's not?" God asked.

"Resolutions? Resisting temptation?" I suggested.

"Perhaps," God said. "Remember when I had someone tell you that 'the worst form of deception is self-deception'?" God asked.

"Vaguely," I mumbled.

"Just a little bit of wisdom I thought I'd share with you through him," God said. "Remember how you felt?"

"I didn't like it," I said, not looking up. God didn't say anything. Sometimes I think God's 'judgment' is God simply giving us the time and space to think about things and come to see the truth — his truth — on our own.

I sighed. "He was right — I'd been kidding myself about something I'd done wrong and was trying to make it look like something it really wasn't," I admitted, burning with shame at the memory.

"Couldn't resist doing that?" God asked gently. "Doing things your own way always tastes *so* good, doesn't it? But you always end up putting on weight. The weight of sin — the anxiety of broken relationships with me and your fellow human beings — that's weight you might want to resolve to lose. The burning feeling you're enjoying right now is what some theologians might call the fires of purgatory. Think of it as burning off a few pounds worth of sin, Tim. Oh, and any time you think you might want help resisting temptation, just call!"

I told God I'd make that my New Year's resolution.

God smiled and said with a wink, "How about we make that your *goal*."

Questions For Discussion

1. Describe a resolution you've made but found difficult to keep? What made it so hard?
2. In what ways do you deceive yourself? Is it really deception? If not, what is it?

Acceptance

A while ago I attended a seminar about pastoral care in healthcare settings. I listened eagerly as the presenters used fascinating personal experiences to illustrate their points. There's one in particular that I'd like to share with you though, because it changed my mind about what it means for a story to have a happy ending.

The doctor who told us the story described a woman in his care who was dying of inoperable cancer. All possible remedies had been exhausted, and he needed to tell her that there was nothing more that could be done for her. He wasn't looking forward to it, because the woman was demanding, critical and manipulative, and had been that way during the entire course of her treatment.

As he entered her room, he could see the look of cold fear on her face. Something about the way he approached her told her what he was going to say, and she didn't let him begin.

"I want you to promise me something doctor," she said, fixing him with her eyes.

"What's that?" he asked uncomfortably.

"I want you to promise me that you won't let me die," she said, gripping his hand with her icy fingers.

"I told her as gently as possible that I couldn't promise her that. We had done everything that could've been done, and there was nothing left to do. I told her she would die soon, though I couldn't say exactly when. In that moment, I wondered if her fear of death had been any part of the reason for her behavior during treatment."

"She began to speak, but something made me grip her hand tightly and I urged her to accept that reality. 'I'm not asking you to like it,' I said. 'Acceptance doesn't mean that what's happening to you is what you want to have happen, that it's good, or bad or anything in between. You don't have to make a quality or "justice" judgment about it at all, let alone feel that anyone, least of all you, has failed somehow. We're past the point where anyone's performance has any meaning," I said. 'You need to acknowledge that what's happening is indeed happening, and it's happening to you, now. That's all acceptance is — and right now, it's everything you've got. For my part, if I can promise you anything that does have meaning, I will promise that I will not leave you alone, or let you suffer pain if I can help it.'"

"She continued to stare at me, but her hand gripped mine less tightly than before. I told her that although nothing more could be done for her body medically, in accepting her situation, she would see that all kinds of things would become possible for her as a person and as a spirit incarnated at that moment in a dying body.

There was nothing more I could say, so I mumbled 'I'm sorry,' turned and left the room, feeling as if I had failed her in her hour of greatest need."

"I returned the next day and found someone I almost didn't recognize. The nurses remarked that she had become a joy to serve, asking questions and trading little stories with them. She was the same way with me, too. It was as if the person I'd been accustomed to seeing had died and left. I got the awesome feeling that I was staring at the raw, beautiful soul of a person who had been liberated from the fear of death and had accepted life writ large."

"A few days later she passed on, I'm told, with a peaceful smile on her face."

Questions For Discussion

1. What is so difficult about acceptance?
2. What can help us turn the corner when something difficult has to be accepted?
3. What might a prayer of acceptance sound like?

Harmony

From time to time, I get together with my friend Pete and we play clarinet duets. He's much better than I am, but he's also kind and patient enough to play at my level. More often than not it sounds pretty good, provided we've been practicing. If we haven't been, it sounds, shall we say, "interesting."

One day not too long ago, God dropped in unexpectedly (it's always like that, isn't it?), and asked me how the music was coming along.

"Oh, it's fine," I lied.

"Been practicing, Tim?" God asked.

"When I can," I explained, "...often enough."

"How often is that?" God wanted to know.

Coming to my senses, I realized I'd better stop trying to hide and confess.

"Not very often," I admitted.

"What does it sound like when you play but don't practice?"

"It sounds like mass murder in a chicken coop," I said. "Is that why you're here?"

"Actually, I'm more interested in harmony, Tim," God said.

"Isn't harmony music?" I asked.

"The harmony I care about is the harmony between me and my creation," God said. "And between all the wonderful creatures I've loved into existence. I care deeply about harmony between us all."

"Is there a problem?" I asked.

"Let's not phrase it that way, Tim," God explained. "Problems just get solved. It's more like there are opportunities."

"For improvement?" I asked.

"Nope — for growth. Think about it. One creature's "improvement" might require another creature's suffering. The opportunities I mean are the opportunities within disharmony that lead to growth and more perfect harmony."

"I don't get it, God," I said plaintively.

"Okay then, Tim," let's start simply," God said. "What does it sound like when you or Pete plays the wrong note?"

"Like a train that just came off the tracks."

"Right. The disharmony's pretty obvious, wouldn't you agree?"

"Amen."

"Don't get holy on me when I'm trying to explain something to you, Tim," God said. "Oh, sorry, God," I said, and God continued.

"Is there any point in trying to hide disharmony?" God asked.

I laughed. "That would be like trying to hide a freshly shrunken head on top of a birthday cake, God."

"Yes — something like that," God said with a grimace.

"Then what do you do?" God asked.

"Well, we replay the passage slowly until we get the notes and timing right. Sometimes we don't know what to do. Maybe there's a better fingering to use, or sometimes it's just plain difficult and we make notes to ourselves to practice. Next time we play, it'll probably sound better, but you never really know."

"Do you think life's a bit like that, too, Tim?" God asked.

"Oh, now I see, God — I think," I said. "But life is crazy — some folks really DO try to hide the disharmony and even keep it secret. How can they ever get the song of their lives right if they never admit that they'd ever gotten it wrong?"

"You teach statistics, Tim. What would you say the probability of that is?" "Zero," I said. God nodded, maybe in agreement, but perhaps it was something else.

"You have faith in me, too, I happen to know. Suppose they come to their senses and decide to practice the harmony I care deeply about, and to practice it in my presence. What would you say about the probability then?"

I laughed. "100%!" I said, and we smiled happily at each other.

"Amen," said God and we played a quiet duet of prayer together.

Questions For Discussion

1. How can we practice harmony?
2. What is so hard about admitting disharmony? How might we pray about that?

Something Big

You never know when you'll be called upon to do something big. Let me tell you a little story about that.

Next Monday's the Boston Marathon, and I'll be heading up to Hopkinton, Massachusetts, again, as I have for several years now. I don't run in the marathon but about thirty ham radio operators including me help people park cars, figure out where to go and respond to the occasional emergency.

A couple of years ago, it was raining as I left home. The rain got worse and worse as I got closer to Hopkinton, and by the time I got there, a full-blown nor'easter was howling along the entire race route.

The way the marathon usually works is that all the runners gather first in the athlete's village, which is on the sports fields at Hopkinton High School. The wheelchair racers start first. Then the elite runners are called, followed by the first wave (serious runners) and second wave (people like me).

It was so rainy though, that the officials herded everyone into the high school. I was stationed at the gym, by the door through which everyone came in or went out. After a while, I got a message to have a Boston Athletic Club person start sending people to the corrals, out of which they begin to run the race. I asked how I'd know who a BAC person was and was told they wore distinctive yellow jackets.

There was only one such individual in sight, so I walked up and gave him the message. I was met with a blank stare. I repeated the message, but there was still no response — just a pained kind of look on the man's face. Then he said *"Ich spreche nur ein bisschen englisch,"* and I realized that we had a big problem on our hands. I called it back in, and after hearing some distressed, muffled mumbling on the other end of the radio, the dispatcher said, "Then *you* start the race."

Me? Start the Boston Marathon? Well, okay. I can do that. I commandeered a couple of bemused policemen and off we went, hollering for folks to head on down to the corrals, wishing them well. I watched in awe as several thousand people followed our orders and marched off into the rain.

You could've done that too. Anyone could've. No question.

I was telling this story to God the other day, and he seemed to enjoy hearing it.

"How would you like to be involved in getting something much bigger under way, Tim?"

I asked God what he meant.

"I'd like you to help people to come to know and love me."

I told God I wasn't sure I could do that. I didn't know how.

"There's nothing you have to know, Tim," God said, "And the less you think you know, the better. All you really have to do is show up, smile and let me work through you. What was it that Saint Francis of Assisi said 'Preach always — if necessary, use words.' I'll take care of the details — all I want you to do is to move out and start the race. You can do that, Tim. Anyone can. No question."

Questions For Discussion

1. From what "big things" have you shied away from in your life, if any?
2. What might you choose to do for God if you knew for sure that God would always be with you? Given the fact that God always is with us, what holds us back?

Familiarity

I was talking with the father of one of our friends who hails from Vermont a few years ago, and the topic turned to the notorious eccentricities of certain folks from the northeast.

"Sometimes I'm struck by how hard it can be to get to know someone in this neck of the woods," I remarked at one point.

My friend's dad listened politely and then asked if he could tell me a story. I said "Sure." Here's how it went:

"About thirty years ago, this fellow from New York bought the farm across the road from mine. I hadn't asked him to do that, but he did it anyway and I decided I'd just mind my own business; I never said anything to him."

I thought maybe there was something about the man that irritated my friend's father, so I asked him what his neighbor was like.

"Don't know," he said.

"Don't you ever talk with each other?" I asked.

"Why?" he wanted to know. "What does he know that I don't?"

"Isn't he friendly?" I inquired.

"Oh, he's friendly enough," he said. "Always waving."

"You had to have spoken to your neighbor," I exclaimed incredulously. "Come on now, what are your conversations like?"

"Never had one," my friend's father insisted. As I started to say something, he interrupted me and corrected himself:

"...except for once last year."

"Oh, do tell me about it," I urged him.

"I was in the post office just trying to mail something. There was a line and I had to wait. He came in and stood behind me. Next thing I know he tapped me on the shoulder. 'What?' I asked. Then he said: 'I don't mean to be a pest,' but I knew he really didn't mean that. Having him just being around was pest enough for me. Then he said again, staring me in the eye like I'd done something to him, 'I don't mean to be a pest, but when do you people around here decide whether you're going to accept someone or not?' I stared back at him and said, 'At your funeral.'"

I was telling that story to God the other day, expecting that God would find it amusing, but God didn't.

"Folks treat me like that sometimes, too," God said.

I felt a little sad for God just then, but God said:

"Don't feel sad. I love them anyway. Sometimes I just wait and wait. So many people put off becoming friends with me until…"

"Their funeral?" I interrupted.

"No, it doesn't take quite that long most of the time," God said.

"Why do people put it off?" I asked.

God laughed and said, "There are so many things that get in the way. Some folks just plain don't see. Others are too busy with all the other interesting gifts with which I shower them in life. Still others are afraid of me, can you imagine? And some make up a very strange image of me in their own minds and become friends with their image instead of with me."

"Weird," I remarked.

"We're just scratching the surface here, Tim," God said.

"Does this bother you?" I asked.

"No," God said. "Everyone always gets 100% of my love, all the time. Surely you know by now that I never hold back. The extent to which my lovely people get to enjoy what's been given to them gets back to what your friend's father said: whose business are they minding — theirs or mine? To be involved in loving, serving and sharing; to forgive and be forgiven — that's so much of the business I'm in. Be like that and we can be friends! Be like that and have life to the fullest!" I took all of that in and ruminated for a bit. Then I asked:

"I'd like to be more than just friends, God. Can it ever be more than that?"

God looked at me with love and said with a wink: ""Sure Tim — after your funeral."

Questions For Discussion

1. What keep us from familiarity with God?
2. What can be more than just being friends with God?

The Forgotten Icon

Praying with icons is a time-honored tradition within Catholic and Eastern Christian spirituality. As St. John Damascene pointed out in his repudiation of iconoclasm in the 8th century, those who pray with icons pray not to the material icons themselves but rather about the spiritual realities the icons represent. As material representations of spiritual realities though, the very existence of icons tells us something deeply true about the mystery of incarnation.

Guidance about icons generally suggests that we use icons representing the Trinity, Jesus, or one of the saints. I'd like to suggest that there is another very powerful icon that everyone has and that most forget. It's your baby picture. No other image conveys that mysterious incarnational message quite as personally.

When I told my wife I wanted to find a baby picture I could use as an icon, she protested.

"Icons have to be of God or of a saint," she said. "You're neither. Nor am I."

"If we think our destiny isn't to be saints," I replied, "I suspect that we'll eventually discover there are vanishingly few attractive alternatives."

"I meant we're not saints yet," my wife explained.

"But maybe in God's eyes," I replied, "we never really left home."

My wife knows where conversations go when I start talking like that, so she promised to help me find a baby picture, which we eventually did.

"Look," I said, after we'd found a charming black-and-white snapshot of cherubic little me lying on a blanket. "That's St. Timothy at the dawn of his creation, when he was a brand new, fabulously unique expression of God's love, destined simply to love and to be loved."

"It's from a time before he knew he was a guy or a girl," I continued, "Before he knew he was black or white, or any particular nationality; before he could speak any language; before he knew much about his parents, siblings or anyone else for that matter; before he'd experienced being cherished or abused by anyone; and I think you'll agree he rather obviously hasn't created himself — he's not his own idea."

"Look at how absolutely helpless, completely dependent, defenseless and utterly vulnerable he is! He doesn't look particularly threatening, does he? All he expects is to give and receive love. How could anyone ever want to hurt him? It's strange to think that little person is God's image and likeness, but there it is. Maybe 'almighty' means something different than what we think."

"Perhaps," my wife said. "But you're a lot different from that little baby now. What's your explanation?"

"Life," I replied. "Both real and imagined, chosen and imposed."

She took that in and then asked, "Why pray with something that doesn't accurately represent you anymore?"

"Because it really does," I replied. "To gaze at that picture is to gaze at God's original and never-ending intention for you and me. Look at that smile! I was born into delight. God had to have been delighting in me, too. Something within me tells me it was always that way and will always be that way, no matter what. Why would we ever want to disconnect from delight?"

We paused silently for a moment, as my wife contemplated my baby picture and I thought over what she had said.

"You're probably right, dear," I said eventually. "I suppose pictures from later in life could also serve as icons, but then we'd be looking at something other than our origin and our prayer might be quite different."

"I wish I had a cute baby picture like that," my wife said. "There's something warm and beautiful in gazing at pristine, innocent love. I think we lost all of my own pictures in the last move."

"You could always use mine, or anyone else's for that matter," I offered. "Everyone's baby picture tells the same tale."

"Your baby icon's growing on me," my wife continued after a bit. "What was that line from the poem you read to me when we were dating about the end of all our wandering being to return to where we'd started and understanding it for the first time?"

"Something by T.S. Eliot, but I don't remember exactly," I replied.

"It's funny how looking at a picture of you then reminds me of something about you now," my wife mused. "It's almost as if I can sense the movements of God's finger in our lives. Just staring at little you makes me think of those gospel passages about children. Doesn't Jesus say some place that unless we become like little children, we can't enter the kingdom of Heaven?"

We gazed quietly at the baby picture together. "Yes, lovely," I agreed. "I think we're staring directly at what that means. Maybe when we're doing things that exclude or prevent us from embracing the reality of our being expressions of God's love, we're busy with things that are outside the kingdom of Love... I mean, 'of God.'"

My wife nodded in agreement and said, "Look at the picture. All that's there is love. Maybe that's what 'purity of heart' means, too. All the pure of heart ever see is love; all we see everywhere and in everyone is God."

We gently put the icon down in our prayer spot in our family room, next to the creche, in the shadow of our crucifix. Then we held hands and moved into the kitchen to make dinner together.

My wife turned and gave me a kiss. "My inner baby loves your inner baby, Tim," she said with a smile, "and the God who made us both. Glad we were incarnated together! Let's make a habit of praying with our new icon."

Questions For Discussion

1. What thoughts go through your mind when you look at and pray with your own baby picture?
2. What was God's original intention for you?
3. How does love manifest itself for different people? What does that tell you about judgment? What does that tell you about God?

Music

Be and See
Contemplative Harmony at its Finest

Dcn. Tim

Oh, all right, so it's not really music, but that's clearly not the point, is it? Back in the Middle Ages, a monk somewhere declared that he had actually heard the music of the spheres one evening, after vespers. Chances are that he was mistaken.

There's no mistaking the gift of contemplative prayer, though. Traveling from our head to our heart, through the depths of our innermost being we come out, not on "the other side," whatever that might be, but into a vast field of seeing — a brilliant field of understanding that is both familiar and utterly new.

Index

This is where the stories showed up in the homilies. If it's useful at all, it's perhaps just that you might see connections similar to those I saw at the time. I hope that if you use the stories, you make them your own. Mix and match to your heart's content, and by all means add your own experiences to them. They're nothing more than seeds that happen to have fallen on your infinitely fertile soil.

By Title Story	Sunday	Lectionary Readings
Miracle	4 Advent A	Matt. 1:8-24
You Look Just Like Jesus	Proper 8/13 Ordinary A	Matt. 10:37-42
Transfiguration	Transfiguration A	Matt. 17:1-9
Satisfaction of the Deep	2 Lent A	Matt. 17:1-9
It's Not Fair!	Proper 20/25 Ordinary A	Matt. 20:1-16a
Where Was God?	Proper 24/29 Ordinary A	Matt. 22:15-21
Pinocchio	Proper 25/30 Orddinary A	Matt. 22:34-40
Repentance	3 Ordinary A	Matt. 4:12-23
Exorcism	4 Ordinary B	Mark 1:21-28
Hospice Visit	Proper 2/7 Ordinary B	Mark 2:1-12
Abuse	Proper 21/26 Ordinary B	Mark 9:38-43, 45, 47-48
Digital Possession	Proper 23/28 Ordinary B	Mark 10:17-30
Servant Leadership	Proper 24/29 Ordinary B	Mark 10:35-45
Palm Sunday	Palm Sunday B	Mark 14:1-15, 47
Blessing	Solemnity of Mary ABC	Luke 2:16-21
Joy And Happiness	3 Advent C	Luke 3:10-18
Chosen	5 Ordinary C	Luke 5:1-11
Forgiving Enemies	Proper 2/7 Ordinary C	Luke 6:27-38

Aneurysm	Proper 9/14 Ordinary C	Luke 10:1-9
Your Worst Nightmare	3 Lent C	Luke 13:1-9
Snakes	4 Lent B	John 3:14-21
Wisdom	Proper 14/19 Ordinary B	John 6:41-51
Messages	4 Easter A	John 10:1-10, 27-30
The Good Shepherd	4 Easter ABC	John 10:1-10, 27-30
Cannibals, Magic	Corpus Christi B	John 18:33b-37
Taz	Divine Mercy	John 20:19-31
Making A Name	Pentecost A	John 20:19-23

www.ingramcontent.com/pod-product-compliance
Lightning Source LLC
Chambersburg PA
CBHW020931180426
43192CB00035B/334